Contents

D1465185

References in these Notes are to the
Arden Shakespeare: Romeo and Juliet,
but as references are also given to particular
acts and scenes, the Notes may be used with
any edition of the play.

Preface

This student revision aid is based on the principle that in any close examination of Shakespeare's plays 'the text's the thing'. Seeing a performance, or listening to a tape or record of a performance, is essential and is in itself a valuable and stimulating experience in understanding and appreciation. However, a real evaluation of Shakespeare's greatness, of his universality and of the nature of his literary and dramatic art, can only be achieved by constant application to the texts of the plays themselves. These revised editions of Brodie's Notes are intended to supplement that process through detailed critical commentary.

The first aim of each book is to fix the whole play in the reader's mind by providing a concise summary of the plot, relating it back, where appropriate, to its source or sources. Subsequently the book provides a summary of each scene, followed by *critical comments*. These may convey its importance in the dramatic structure of the play, creation of atmosphere, indication of character development, significance of figurative language etc, and they will also explain or paraphrase difficult words or phrases and identify meaningful references. At the end of each act revision questions in ascending order of difficulty are set to test the student's specific and broad understanding and appreciation of the play.

An extended critical commentary follows this scene by scene analysis. This embraces such major elements as characterization, imagery, the use of blank verse and prose, soliloquies and other aspects of the play which the editor considers need close attention. The paramount aim is to send the reader back to the text. The book concludes with a series of revision questions which require a detailed knowledge of the play; the first of these has notes by the editor of what *might* be included in a written answer. The intention is to stimulate and to guide; the whole emphasis of this commentary is to encourage the student's *involvement* in the play, to develop disciplined critical responses and thus promote personal enrichment through the imaginative experience of our greatest writer.

Graham Handley

Shakespeare and the Elizabethan playhouse

William Shakespeare was born in Stratford-upon-Avon in 1564, and there are reasons to suppose that he came from a relatively prosperous family. He was probably educated at Stratford Grammar School and, at the age of eighteen, married Anne Hathaway, who was twenty-six. They had three children, a girl born shortly after their marriage, followed by twins in 1585 (the boy died in 1596). It seems likely that Shakespeare left for London shortly after a company of visiting players had visited Stratford in 1585, for by 1592 – according to the jealous testimony of one of his fellow-writers Robert Greene – he was certainly making his way both as actor and dramatist. The theatres were closed because of the plague in 1593; when they reopened Shakespeare worked with the Lord Chamberlain's Men, later the King's Men, and became a shareholder in each of the two theatres with which he was most closely associated, the Globe and the Blackfriars. He later purchased New Place, a considerable property in his home town of Stratford, to which he retired in 1611; there he entertained his great contemporary Ben Jonson (1572–1637) and the poet Michael Drayton (1563–1631). An astute businessman, Shakespeare lived comfortably in the town until his death in 1616.

This is a very brief outline of the life of our greatest writer, for little more can be said of him with certainty, though the plays – and poems – are living witness to the wisdom, humanity and many-faceted nature of the man. He was both popular and successful as a dramatist, perhaps less so as an actor. He probably began work as a dramatist in the late 1580s, by collaborating with other playwrights and adapting old plays, and by 1598 Francis Meres was paying tribute to his excellence in both comedy and tragedy. His first original play was probably *Love's Labour's Lost* (1590) and while the theatres were closed during the plague he wrote his narrative poems *Venus and Adonis* (1593) and *The Rape of Lucrece* (1594). The sonnets were almost certainly written in the 1590s though not published until 1609; the first 126 seem to be addressed to a young man who was his friend and patron, while the rest are concerned with the 'dark lady'.

The dating of Shakespeare's plays has exercised scholars ever since the publication of the First Folio (1623), which listed them as comedies, histories and tragedies. It seems more important to look at them chronologically as far as possible, in order to trace Shakespeare's considerable development as a dramatist. The first period, say to the middle of the 1590s, included such plays as *Love's Labour's Lost*, *The Comedy of Errors*, *Richard III*, *The Taming of the Shrew*, *Romeo and Juliet* and *Richard II*. These early plays embrace the categories listed in the First Folio, so that Shakespeare the craftsman is evident in his capacity for variety of subject and treatment. The next phase includes *A Midsummer's Night's Dream*, *The Merchant of Venice*, *Henry IV Parts 1 and 2*, *Henry V* and *Much Ado About Nothing*, as well as *Julius Caesar*, *As You Like It* and *Twelfth Night*. These are followed, in the early years of the 17th century, by his great tragic period: *Hamlet*, *Othello*, *King Lear* and *Macbeth*, with *Antony and Cleopatra* and *Coriolanus* belonging to 1607–09. The final phase embraces the romances (1610–13), *Cymbeline*, *The Tempest* and *The Winter's Tale* and the historical play *Henry VIII*.

Each of these revision aids will place the individual text under examination in the chronology of the remarkable dramatic output that spanned twenty years from the early 1590s to about 1613. The practical theatre for which Shakespeare wrote and acted derived from the inn courtyards in which performances had taken place, the few playhouses in his day being modelled on their structure. They were circular or hexagonal in shape, allowing the balconies and boxes around the walls full view of the stage. This large stage, which had no scenery, jutted out into the pit, the most extensive part of the theatre, where the poorer people – the 'groundlings' – stood. There was no roof (though the Blackfriars, used from 1608 onwards, was an indoor theatre) and thus bad weather meant no performance. Certain plays were acted at court, and these private performances normally marked some special occasion. Costumes, often rich ones, were used, and music was a common feature, with musicians on or under the stage; this sometimes had additional features, for example a trapdoor to facilitate the entry of a ghost. Women were barred by law from appearing on stage, and all female parts were played by boy actors; this undoubtedly explains the many instances in Shakespeare where a woman has to conceal her identity by disguising

herself as a man, e.g. Rosalind in *As You Like It*, Viola in *Twelfth Night*.

Shakespeare and his contemporaries often adapted their plays from sources in history and literature, extending an incident or a myth or creating a dramatic narrative from known facts. They were always aware of their own audiences, and frequently included topical references, sometimes of a satirical flavour, which would appeal to – and be understood by – the groundlings as well as their wealthier patrons who occupied the boxes. Shakespeare obviously learned much from his fellow dramatists and actors, being on good terms with many of them. Ben Jonson paid generous tribute to him in the lines prefaced to the First Folio of Shakespeare's plays:

Thou art a monument without a tomb,
And art alive still, while thy book doth live
And we have wits to read, and praise to give.

Among his contemporaries were Thomas Kyd (1558–94) and Christopher Marlowe (1564–93). Kyd wrote *The Spanish Tragedy*, the revenge motif here foreshadowing the much more sophisticated treatment evident in *Hamlet*, while Marlowe evolved the 'mighty line' of blank verse, a combination of natural speech and elevated poetry. The quality and variety of Shakespeare's blank verse owes something to the innovatory brilliance of Marlowe but carries the stamp of individuality, richness of association, technical virtuosity and, above all, the genius of imaginative power.

The texts of Shakespeare's plays are still rich sources for scholars, and the editors of these revision aids have used the Arden editions of Shakespeare, which are regarded as pre-eminent for their scholarly approach. They are strongly recommended for advanced students, but other editions, like The New Penguin Shakespeare, The New Swan, The Signet are all good annotated editions currently available. A reading list of selected reliable works on the play being studied is provided at the end of each commentary and students are advised to turn to these as their interest in the play deepens.

Literary terms used in these notes

Alliteration Several words close together starting with the same letter: 'Stand *t*iptoe on the *m*isty *m*ountain *t*ops.'

Antithesis Ideas which though opposites are placed close to one another for contrast: 'Here's much to do with hate, but more with love/Why then, O brawling love, O loving hate' (I,1,173–4).

Blank verse The normal metre used in Elizabethan plays, each line having ten syllables, technically known as the iambic pentameter and modelled originally on Latin verse: 'Rebellious subjects, enemies to peace' (I,1,79).

Couplet Two lines of verse rhymed as a pair: 'O, she is rich in beauty; only poor/That, when she dies, with beauty dies her store'.

Dramatic irony A device much used by dramatists; there are two main types. **a)** Where a character does something that he thinks will produce a certain result only to find that it has the opposite result or comes about in a way he had not anticipated (e.g. Friar Laurence marries Romeo and Juliet in the hope that it will end the feud between their families). **b)** Where a character says something in total ignorance that he is in fact speaking the truth, but where the audience can see the double meaning: 'Methinks I see thee, now thou art so low,/As one dead in the bottom of a tomb' (III,5,55) – next time Juliet sees Romeo he really is dead.

Irony Where the real meaning is the opposite of that apparently expressed. 'Well, thou hast comforted me marvellous much' (III,5,230): Juliet means that the Nurse has not comforted her at all.

Metaphor A compressed comparison without the use of 'like' or 'as': 'It is the East and Juliet is the sun!' (II,2,3). It is not really the east; Romeo is saying that the appearance of Juliet is like the sun rising.

Oxymoron Contradictory words placed next to one another 'Beautiful tyrant, fiend angelical,/Dove-feather'd raven, wolvish-ravening lamb!' (III,2,76).

Pun or quibble Two words that sound the same but have different meanings:

Romeo . . . and I am *done.*
Mercutio Tut, *dun's* the mouse   (I,4,39)

Rhetoric The art of speaking, taught to every Elizabethan schoolboy. They learned how to give their points maximum impact, how to develop an argument, how to illustrate a point with reference to other works (often in Latin or Greek). Rhetorical language is frequent in the play, e.g. 'Rebellious subjects, enemies to peace,/Profaners of this neighbour-stained steel' (I,1,79–80). All three descriptions really mean the same thing; they are included to give the prince's speech impact.

'Love is a smoke made with the fume of sighs;

Being purg'd, a fire sparkling in lovers' eyes;

Being vex'd, a sea nourished with lovers' tears' (I,1,188–90). Here Romeo's thoughts on love are elaborated according to a fixed pattern of repeated phrases.

Simile A comparison which includes the words 'like' or 'as': 'darkness fleckled like a drunkard reels' (II,2,190), 'The brightness of her cheek would shame those stars/As daylight doth a lamp' (II,2,19–20).

The play

Plot

The background of the story is the long-standing feud between two families of Verona, the Capulets and the Montagues. The play opens with a brawl in which the Prince is forced to intervene to stop the rioting: he threatens to put to death any who should dare revive the feud. We then meet Romeo, son of Montague, who hears of the brawl from his cousin Benvolio. Romeo is suffering the pains of unrequited love though his friends, first Benvolio and then Mercutio, regard this as little more than a ridiculous infatuation. Hearing of a feast at Capulet's house they determine to attend it in disguise so that Romeo may be able to judge his lady's beauty alongside that of the other ladies of Verona.

Meanwhile Paris, a young nobleman, has asked Capulet for his daughter Juliet's hand in marriage, only to be told that at thirteen she is far too young to be married and that he should wait for two years. Lady Capulet has suggested the idea of marriage to Juliet who greets it dutifully. In the middle of the feast Romeo meets Juliet, is immediately attracted to her and she to him; however, they soon realize the great obstacles that stand in the way of any possible relationship. Romeo climbs into Capulet's garden and overhears Juliet's confession of love for him; he makes known his presence and they decide on a secret marriage. With the help of Friar Laurence they are married next day.

Mercutio and Benvolio meet Tybalt, nephew to Capulet, who is obsessed by the stain on the family honour caused by Romeo's secret presence at the feast, and they quarrel. Romeo arrives and attempts unsuccessfully to defuse the quarrel, and in the ensuing fight Mercutio is killed by accident. In a compulsive desire to avenge his friend's death, Romeo draws on Tybalt and kills him; the entry of the Prince stops the fight, and Romeo is sentenced to banishment for his part in it. Early next morning Romeo leaves for Mantua after spending the night with Juliet.

Capulet changes his mind and decides to accept Paris's request for marriage to his daughter immediately. Faced with her opposition to the match, he abruptly loses his good humour and tyrannically insists on the marriage taking place within two days. Juliet asks the Friar for his advice, and he tells her to agree to the match, but gives her a potion and tells her to drink it the night before the wedding; it will give her the appearance of death for forty-two hours. His intention is to warn Romeo, who will then rescue her from the vault and take her to Mantua; their wedding can then be announced at a suitable time. Juliet obeys and drinks the potion.

Unfortunately the Friar's message does not reach Romeo and he hears independently of Juliet's death. He buys some poison and goes to the Capulet tomb intending to see her once more before killing himself. Outside the tomb he meets Paris; they fight, and Paris is killed. After seeing Juliet, Romeo takes the poison and dies; almost immediately Juliet wakes and finds Romeo dead at her side. She takes a dagger from his belt, stabs herself, and dies too. The story is told by the Friar and Paris's page, and the tragedy finally reconciles the two feuding families.

Source

Hardly any of Shakespeare's plots are his own. The story of Romeo and Juliet originates as a piece of folklore in Italy and it is impossible to say how old it is. Very similar stories are found in classical times and are known sometimes to have had a basis in fact but were embellished and decorated over the centuries. The tale as we know it assumes recognizable form in 15th and 16th century Italy in one of the many collections of stories called *novelle*. Shakespeare knew many of these and used them as the source stories for a number of his plays.

The immediate source of *Romeo and Juliet*, however, is a long poem by Arthur Brooke, published in 1562, and just over 3000 lines long. Brooke had found it translated from the Italian of Bandello's *novella* into French by Pierre Boaistuau in 1559. It is probable that Shakespeare also read a prose version of Boaistuau's story by William Painter 'The goodly History of the true and constant love between Romeo and Jullietta' in the second volume of his *Palace of Pleasure* (1567). There was also a play which Brooke mentions in his 'Preface to the Reader' though this has not survived. Shakespeare however may have known it though one must remember that he had not been born when

Brooke's poem first appeared, and that when his play appeared the story had been well known for more than thirty years.

Treatment of source

Shakespeare's treatment of his source is infinitely more important than the source itself. Though he follows Brooke's poem very closely at times and must have had a copy of it to hand as he was writing his play, he alters it a good deal, changing the emphasis in various places and introducing new characters. The poem is written in long, rambling couplets, and if Shakespeare's play sometimes reflects this by itself using couplets, he handles the couplets more crisply. For the most part, the poem is so drawn out that, but for Shakespeare, it would have been forgotten completely.

The most immediate difference is that of time. In Brooke's poem the action takes nine months; Shakespeare condenses this into five days. This has the effect of tightening the action considerably, though it also poses some problems. The movement of the play is clearly marked, according to the following timetable:

Sunday The play opens with a street brawl at nine o'clock in the morning. Romeo and Juliet first meet at a party that same night. After the feast Romeo gets into Capulet's garden and talks to Juliet at her window.

Monday They are married in the afternoon. Soon afterwards Romeo kills Tybalt and is banished, but he spends the night with Juliet. Late that night Capulet arranges the marriage with Paris for Thursday morning.

Tuesday As dawn breaks Romeo leaves Juliet. He has no sooner gone than Juliet is told by her parents that she is to marry Paris, and in despair she goes to Friar Lawrence's cell. Late that night the wedding is advanced to take place next morning. Before she goes to sleep Juliet takes the Friar's potion.

Wednesday At dawn Juliet is discovered 'dead'. She is taken to the family tomb.

Thursday Romeo hears of Juliet's death and buys poison.

Friday During the very early morning while it is still dark, Romeo comes to the tomb, and the rest of the play takes place before it is fully light.

In thus changing the original time-scheme Shakespeare turns the world of the play into one of frenzied activity. Servants fight as soon as they see one another, lovers fall in love immediately and want to be married within a day; even when a marriage is approved by older people, it has to be celebrated within two days; and the shock of the death of the lovers changes a feud of long-standing into reconciliation in a moment. We are always aware that the 'mad blood' is stirring, yet at the same time Shakespeare is reluctant to give up all the advantages of spreading out the story over Brooke's nine months. Thus we hear about damping the fire as the room is grown too hot, yet only a day later Benvolio talks about the day being hot. The Nurse tells Romeo that she angers Juliet 'sometimes' and speaks as if she has known Romeo for a long time – according to Juliet she has praised him 'above compare so many thousand times' yet in fact she has known him for only a couple of days. Again, we see Juliet as almost a little girl in Act I and as a mature woman only two days later; if Romeo has spent only a day in Mantua, he has got to know the shopkeepers and the whereabouts of the shops remarkably quickly!

In Shakespeare's play two important characters are the Nurse and Mercutio, both of them little more than names in the original story. They are introduced for contrast – Mercutio with Romeo and the Nurse with Juliet – and they are two of the most memorable characters in the play.

Juliet's age is reduced from fifteen to thirteen; we hear about this in Act I Scene 3 where her youth is mentioned in order to emphasize her freshness and innocence. It is not mentioned in the latter part of the play where we see her maturing before our eyes, and where Shakespeare seems to have thought of her as being distinctly older.

The change that has taken place between Brooke's meandering couplets and Shakespeare's assured verse is astounding. In Brooke we are still in the world of medieval romance where the whole story is told in the third person; we are constantly reminded of stories such as Chaucer's *Troilus and Criseyde*. Shakespeare writes with a freshness that fills out the wooden characters of the original and turns them into real, closely-observed people, and he does so in verse that at its best is so memorable that it has become part of the language, quoted as one of the world's definitive plays about love.

Date

The first allusion to a performance of *Romeo and Juliet* in contemporary literature occurs in 1598 when John Marston refers to a production which took place at The Curtain. Other evidence indicates that the play cannot have been written later than 1596, as the first edition of the play was printed by John Danter in 1597 and refers to many performances as already having taken place. This edition was pirated – that is, published without the authorization of Shakespeare's company – and is textually unreliable; pirated copies are known to have been scribbled down by members of the audience, or to have been dictated by actors bribed to repeat their parts, but who were unable to remember other characters' parts with any great accuracy.

The earliest possible date for the play is indicated by pieces which Shakespeare himself has borrowed from other authors, notably Samuel Daniel and Eliot's *Ortho-Epia*. These date from 1592 and 1593. The probable date for *Romeo and Juliet* is therefore 1594-5, and indications are that it was written soon after *Love's Labour's Lost*.

Scene summaries, critical commentary, textual notes and revision questions

Prologue

The Prologue is an introduction to the play, originally imitated from the classical plays which were the models for most playwrights before Shakespeare. It is written as a sonnet – a poem of 14 lines with a set form and pattern of rhyme – which was universally popular in the 1590s; *Romeo and Juliet* contains several examples.

The Chorus in Greek plays was a collection of actors who commented on the action of the play, but in Elizabethan plays its function is usually filled by one actor.

ancient grudge Long-lasting quarrel.
break to new mutiny Fall into renewed strife.
civil blood makes civil hands unclean Blood shed in civil war stains the hands of people normally civilized.
fatal loins Reproductive organs destined to produce issue fated for misfortune.
star-cross'd The stars were destined to bring about this misfortune. The first of a number of times where the influence of the stars is indicated as a prime cause of the tragedy.
Whose ... overthrows Whose ill-fated tragic struggles.
but Except for.
What here shall miss Whatever is lacking in this account.

Act I Scene 1

The opening of the play has an immediate impact upon the audience, as within thirty lines we are in the middle of violent action in the shape of a renewed episode in the long-standing feud between two of the leading families of Verona – the Capulets and the Montagues. The servants of each of the families are involved as much as their masters, though they seem to be going through the motions of renewing the quarrel until Tybalt arrives to put some passion into the fight. Capulet and Montague seem to join in with enthusiasm, although the citizens are weary of the constant violence – 'Down with the Capulets! Down with the Montagues!'. The Prince enters and his authority immediately puts an end to the brawl, threatening both families with death should it break out again, and asking each family to attend him to know his 'farther pleasure in this case'.

Benvolio is in the middle of an account of the fight when Lady Montague inquires after her son Romeo, only to be told that he has been avoiding everyone. Montague thinks Romeo may be ill, and Benvolio undertakes to try to find the cause of this illness. Romeo appears, full of stylish melancholy in that his love (for Rosaline) is not returned; he will not even reveal her name. Romeo's 'love' has all the attributes of the conventional Elizabethan love-object – she is chaste, and has to be adored from afar by her hopeless and despairing suitor. The conventional quality of Romeo's love is matched by equally conventional language, using comparisons that are only too obvious, and a number of verbal quibbles.

Commentary

The scene is notable for its variety. It moves from fairly mechanical prose to Tybalt's equally mechanical verse; from the Prince's assured and rhetorical lines to Benvolio's lyrical description; and it ends with Romeo's yearning for his love. *Romeo and Juliet* is one of Shakespeare's early plays, but none of his contemporaries have a comparable range and assurance within such a limited space.

carry coals Put up with insults, be treated as the lowest servants.
colliers Coal carriers, famed for their dishonesty.
choler Anger. Within three lines we are presented with what is to be one of the main stylistic features of the play – its puns. We have already collier–choler–collar; two senses of 'draw' and 'move'.
moved Aroused.
dog A low-down fellow from the rival household.
move me to stand Make me stand my ground and fight.
take the wall Get the better of – the strongest walked closest to the wall, as he ran less risk of stepping into rubbish thrown into the street.
weakest goes to the wall A proverbial expression derived from medieval churches which often provided seating along the wall only for the infirm. In this battle of wits, it neatly answers Sampson's statement.
thrust his maids to the wall i.e. sexually assault them.
between . . . men i.e. we will not bring the women into it.
'Tis all one It's all the same to me.

maidenheads Virginity.

sense (1) meaning (2) feeling.

while . . . flesh While I can gain an erection and I am (1) well endowed sexually (2) a fine fellow.

Poor–John A frequent dish at the time – dried and salted hake; poor fare, and certainly unlikely to 'stand'.

back thee (1) support, which Gregory interprets as meaning (2) run away.

take the law of Keep the law on.

list Please.

bite my thumb A very rude gesture in Shakespeare's time.

washing blow Knock-out blow.

heartless hinds (1) cowardly servants (2) female deer unprotected by a stag. Tybalt considers that Benvolio should not attempt to fight men of a rank so much lower than his own.

thy death My sword (which will cause it).

manage Use.

Have at thee Take that!

Clubs, bills, and partisans Cries of London apprentices when embarking on one of their frequent riots. They were all weapons – *bills* being pikes and *partisans* broad-headed spears.

long sword An old-fashioned weapon requiring strength to lift; Lady Capulet suggests that Capulet is not strong enough to do so.

A crutch . . . Lady Capulet is scorning her husband by reminding him of his age.

spite Defiance.

Hold me not . . . This is spoken to his wife.

Profaners . . . steel You commit sacrilege against your weapons by staining them with the blood of your neighbours.

mistemper'd Tempered for an ignoble use.

movèd Angry.

airy word Completely trivial cause.

grave-beseeming ornaments (1) sober and useful tools (2) instruments that they will take to the grave.

Canker'd (1) Rusted (2) Diseased.

abroach Flowing (image of an opened barrel).

by Near.

in the instant At the same time.

hissed him in scorn An onomatopoeic description of the passage of his sword through the air.

part and part Either side.

parted either part Separated the two sides.

sycamore This was associated with disappointed lovers (sick *amour*, from the French for *love*).

ware Aware.

Which . . . found Which was most anxious to find the place where there were fewest people.

humour Inclination (by not following Romeo).

all so soon as As soon as ever.

The . . . bed i.e. dawn breaks (from the classical goddess of the dawn).

heavy Note the contrast with 'light' earlier in the line.

importun'd Questioned him.

his own affections' counsellor Keeps his feelings to himself.

sounding and discovery Being made to reveal himself (image from finding the depth of water beneath a ship).

envious Malignant.

know i.e. what the trouble is.

Enter Romeo Dramatically it is much more effective to 'lead up' to Romeo like this in the conversation of minor characters, than to bring him on the stage at the outset. Here the description has reflected Romeo's youth and freshness; he has also managed to avoid involvement in the brawl.

true shrift A confession.

Is the day so young? Romeo has been up since before dawn and thinks that it is much later.

having When one has it (i.e. a lady's affection).

proof Reality.

muffled Cupid was usually shown with a blindfold over his eyes, but nevertheless managed to hit the target with his arrows.

fray . . . Romeo sees signs of the brawl.

Why then . . . what it is A series of nouns and adjectives which contradict each other and are given the name of oxymorons. They reflect the confusion in Romeo's mind.

serious vanity Heavy emptiness.

no love i.e. none which really satisfies him.

propagate Increase.

love . . . The series of statements that Romeo makes about love are vague, fanciful and bear little relation to the real thing which he is later to experience with Juliet.

coz Cousin – used in Elizabethan times for any relation.

sadness Seriously.

groan Romeo purposely misunderstands 'sadness' to mean what it does today.

ill-urg'd Unkindly used.

I aim'd so near I guessed that.

fair mark Clear target (image from archery).

Dian's wit The knowledge of Diana the Roman goddess of chastity, who can withstand the arrows of the young Cupid.

siege . . . encounter All images from siege warfare, developed from the 'bow' of line 209.

with beauty dies her store Her beauty will die with her – a central idea in Shakespeare's work at this time, particularly in the early sonnets. The facts that Romeo here speaks in couplets adds to the feeling of artificiality.

huge waste i.e. as children will never inherit her beauty.
merit bliss Deserve happiness in heaven.
forsworn Refused.
rul'd Advised.
To call ... more It will only emphasize her exquisite beauty all the more.
passing Surpassingly.
What doth her beauty serve What is the use of her beauty?
pass'd Surpassed.
I'll ... debt I will go on trying to make you forget – until my death if need be.

Act I Scene 2

Capulet is conversing with Paris about the recent brawl. Paris acknowledges the position of both Montague and Capulet, regretting that the feud had lasted so long; he then asks Capulet if he will agree to his marriage to Juliet. Capulet answers that Juliet is too young; she is his only surviving daughter and he will not marry her against her will. If Paris can gain her consent he will add his own. He then says that he is holding a feast at his home that night, invites Paris to attend, and gives a servant a list of guests who are to be invited too.

The servant cannot read and has to search out someone who can; he meets Romeo and Benvolio who are continuing the conversation of Scene 1. Romeo reads the list and is impressed to see the name of his beloved Rosaline included. The servant gives them both a casual invitation to come if they are not Montagues and they both decide to go.

Commentary

The scene contrasts the seriousness of Romeo and Benvolio with the humour of the servant.

bound i.e. to keep the peace.
reckoning Position. Paris is being extremely tactful in view of the Prince's opinion.
saying o'er Repeating.
stranger in the world Innocent of the ways of the world.
the change of fourteen years In Shakespeare's sources Juliet was older. Shakespeare throws constant emphasis on her youth.
wither in their pride Pass by (literally: the flowers of two summers wither).

my earth (a) My lands (b) My heiress.

My will . . . part My permission is less important than her c[...]
is a rather different attitude from that which Capulet displa[...]

And she agreed And if she agrees.

old accustom'd feast One which has long been held at this time.

Earth-treading stars i.e. Beautiful ladies.

well-apparell'd Well-dressed.

limping winter i.e. like an old man who limps away to make way for
spring.

Inherit Receive.

Which . . . in reckoning none When you have seen the variety there,
my daughter (who will be one of them) may be one of those who you
consider worthy of consideration, though she is not one who figures in
the list of accepted beauties.

sirrah A term of address used for inferiors.

Find them . . . In good time The servant's part was apparently played
by a clown; he gets the tools of the various trades thoroughly
confused. His inability to read is a further source of humour.

Tut . . . Benvolio is still impatient with Romeo; his speech is the latter
part (the sestet) of an Elizabethan sonnet. He then presents Romeo
with a succession of paradoxes:

one fire . . . burning A larger fire will consume a smaller one.

one pain . . . anguish A greater pain will make a lesser one seem trivial.

Turn giddy . . . turning Turn giddy and you will be helped by turning
in the opposite direction.

One . . . languish One grief is cured by the depression caused by
another.

Your plantain . . . for that Romeo here makes fun of the remedies for
broken hearts suggested by Benvolio, by countering with one for an
injured leg.

God gi' good e'en May God give you a good evening.

without book By heart.

Ye say honestly The servant here supposes that Romeo has admitted
that he cannot read.

rest you merry Cheers!

County and **Count** are used interchangeably throughout the play.

Rosaline The first time that Romeo's beloved is mentioned in the text
in a way that can identify her as the lady we have heard so much about.

unattainted Impartial.

devout religion Romeo seems to worship Rosaline; he uses the same
image when he first meets Juliet, but at much greater length and with
more concentration.

And these who . . . liars Romeo is referring to the custom of detecting
people suspected of dealing with the devil by putting them in water; if
they floated it was with the devil's help, and they were clearly
('transparent') heretics.

Tut, you saw ... being by You thought she was beautiful as there was no competition present.

Herself ... eye She was like a pair of scales with herself on either side (continuing the same idea but with a different metaphor).

shining at this feast ... We are prepared for the imagery of light that is so much a feature of this play.

And she shall ... best i.e. she who now appears attractive will appear so to only a small degree.

splendour of mine own The splendid beauty of my beloved.

Act I Scene 3

This scene introduces us to the thirteen-year-old Juliet who is called before her mother to learn that her parents are planning to marry her to Paris. Juliet is summoned by her Nurse, who speaks of Juliet's babyhood and childhood in a way that tells us more about herself than it does about Juliet. Lady Capulet steers the conversation in the direction she wants it to take – that of her wish that Juliet should marry. She speaks of Paris in glowing terms, ignoring the Nurse's bawdy comment; Juliet's dutiful reply shows that she is ready to obey her mother's bidding. The pace of the scene is quickened by a servingman who announces that all three ladies are in demand as preparations for the approaching feast are made.

Commentary

Undoubtedly the most remarkable element in this scene is the character of the Nurse, a closely observed portrait and a rewarding one for a mature actress. She is colloquial, repetitive and absolutely frank about herself and her attitude to life. Her speech of over thirty lines gives little information, but conveys a certain butterfly-mindedness that is combined with a motherly protectiveness towards Juliet, shown very well in her tendency to reminisce over her charge's childhood. The Nurse's description of the way in which Juliet was weaned, factually accurate as it no doubt is, is a little crude to be thus gone over in the company of one who would certainly wish such embarrassing memories well forgotten. Her joke about Juliet falling backwards (which Juliet might not understand at the age of thirteen) confirms this coarse side of her nature, which appears as regularly as she does. While she defers to Lady Capulet, her mistress, she clearly has the assurance of an established and trusted retainer.

Lady Capulet's description of Paris is a formal one in the way it acknowledges his merits and in the way it uses one particular image – that of a book, and stretches it out to such an elaborate degree that it is an excellent example of a conceit.

by my maidenhood at twelve year old i.e. she could not swear to her virginity by the time she was thirteen – an indication of how early girls could then be married.

ladybird A pet name but with associations; it also meant 'whore' and the Nurse is disclaiming this secondary meaning for her young mistress. ('God forbid').

Madam I am here Juliet's address to her mother is always formal.

give leave Excuse us.

thou's Thou shalt. 'Thou' is the form of address used between relations or close friends; it could also be used to show contempt. The Nurse uses the more formal 'you'.

counsel Conversation.

teen Sorrow (pun on four*teen*).

Lammas-tide 1 August. Juliet will be fourteen on 31st July.

Susan The Nurse is talking about her dead daughter.

the earthquake There were various earthquakes in England in the 1580s – in addition to any that might have occurred at Verona, so the allusion was topical.

wean'd ... wormwood The Nurse was literally a Nurse to Juliet. Ladies of fashion did not breastfeed their own children and the Nurse had abundant milk from the recent death of Susan. The favoured method of weaning children was to apply a bitter substance ('wormwood') to the nipple.

dug An old (and somewhat coarse) word for 'breast'.

tetchy Bad-tempered.

Shake ... dovehouse The pigeon-house shook (referring to the earthquake earlier in the day).

I trow I assure you.

To bid me trudge To dismiss me (as the main part of her job was finished).

high-lone Unaided.

th' rood The cross on which Christ died.

broke her brow Cut her forehead.

Thou wilt fall backward ... wit i.e. you will be ready for making love.

by my holidame A corruption of 'halidom', holy thing or relic.

it stinted It stopped.

cockerel's stone Testicle.

dispositions Inclinations.

much upon these years About the same age.

of wax i.e. as if modelled in wax – perfect.

Read o'er ... lacks a cover A long image comparing Paris with a book. Two lines later the idea returns in 'gold clasps' (valuable books were often locked in Shakespeare's time) and 'golden story'.

Examine every ... make it fly This is written in couplets. It is hard to make these sound natural on the modern stage, but they are frequent features of Elizabethan plays. The audience of that time liked formality, a feature which we can also see in the balanced lines, e.g. 'fair without the fair within to hide', and which appears in the many sections of dialogue which are written in the form of a sonnet – part or whole.

Women ... men While Lady Capulet speaks of spiritual growth, the only growth which the Nurse recognizes is that resulting from pregnancy.

endart mine eye A conceit deriving from Cupid's arrows ('darts' in the language of the play) which are referred to again in the next line ('make it fly').

Act I Scene 4

Romeo is one of a group of Montagues on the way to Capulet's feast, carrying out the resolve formed at the end of Scene 2. One of the party is Romeo's friend Mercutio.

Commentary

Much of the scene is devoted to developing Romeo's character rather than carrying forward the plot. Romeo is in much the same mood which we have noted in both his appearances so far, but Mercutio gives the play an entirely new touch; his constant puns and flights of fancy make Romeo seem leaden and earthbound. The scene ends with a touch of foreboding from Romeo that the outcome will not be a happy one.

Masquers Men with masks.

Torchbearers ... This would indicate to the audience that the scene took place at night.

this speech i.e. speech of apology (for coming to the ball without a formal invitation) as the next line shows.

The date ... prolixity It is now unfashionable to make such speeches.

Cupid ... scarf Guest disguised as Cupid blindfolded.

Tartar's ... lath Cheap bow in the shape of a lip.

crowkeeper Scarecrow.

without–book From memory.

measure ... will Judge us how they please.

measure them a measure Dance a measure (pun on the previous line).

Give me a torch i.e. I do not want to dance and so will be a torchbearer.

ambling A contemptuous reference to dancing.

heavy . . . light Romeo is rather fond of this punning antithesis – he has used it before in I, 1, 176 and Montague has used it before him at I, 1, 135.

stakes me to the ground An image from bull or bear-baiting.

common bound (1) Ordinary jump (2) Everyday limits (3) A common man tied up.

sore . . . soar Further punning; Romeo also uses the other senses of 'bound' from line 18.

pitch A metaphor from falconry – the height from which a falcon swooped onto its prey.

And to sink . . . tender thing Mercutio perverts Romeo's remarks into a sexual quibble: in order to make love you need to lie on top of the object of your affections and tender parts often suffer.

Prick . . . down Give love back as good as you get and you will defeat it. There is a bawdy quibble on 'prick' and on 'beat love down'.

case Mask.

A visor for a visor i.e. My face is hideous enough not to need a mask.

quote Notice.

beetle brows . . . blush The mask would seem to have prominent eyebrows and red cheeks.

Tickle the senseless rushes . . . The Elizabethan hall had rushes strewn on the floor.

proverb'd with a grandsire phrase Supported by an old man's proverb (that the candle-holder or onlooker sees most of the game).

The game . . . done When gambling, it is always better to quit while still ahead.

dun's the mouse A slang Elizbethan phrase meaning 'keep quiet' hence 'the constable's own word'.

save your reverence A quibble on filth, dung. This meaning came about because the word was used to replace unpleasant things (it means 'excuse my mentioning it').

we burn daylight We are wasting time (from the burning of candles in daylight).

Nay that's not so Romeo perversely takes Mercutio's statement literally. Mercutio's explanation of what he means has the effect of reminding the audience that the scene takes place at night.

Take our good meaning . . . five wits i.e. take the meaning I intended for my good sense is five times more visible in that than it is in one who is merely clever in playing with words.

Queen Mab Spoken of as queen of the Fairies; her name appears in Welsh and Irish folklore.

fairies' midwife One who delivers the dreams of men ('children of an idle brain', line 97).

agate stone The figure cut in the stone of a ring and used as a seal.

long spinners' legs Legs of the crane-fly or daddy-long-legs.

cover The hood of the wagon.

traces Reins.

film Gossamer.

Not half . . . maid Worms were popularly supposed to breed in the fingers of lazy girls.

straight Straightaway.

smelling out a suit Seeking to obtain one from a monarch.

tithe-pig A clergyman was entitled to claim the tenth of any litter of pigs as his 'tithe'.

benefice Church appointment.

breaches Gaps made in defensive walls.

ambuscados Ambushes.

Spanish blades Spanish steel was famous for its quality and the swords of Toledo were especially sought after.

healths . . . deep Never-ending drinking.

Drums The signal for battle.

swears a prayer or two i.e. swearing is so natural to him that he cannot pray without swearing.

bakes Clots.

elf-locks When dirty hair became clotted together it was superstitiously put down to elves, hence 'elf-locks'. It happened only to filthy hair, hence 'foul sluttish hairs'.

untangled Entangled.

This is the hag . . . to bear The fairy appears in the form of a hag who gives girls erotic dreams.

learns Teaches.

good carriage (1) upright bearing (2) able to bear children (3) able to bear a lover.

woos . . . north i.e. blows warmly on the northern wastes.

blows us from ourselves Diverts us from our purpose – to go to the party.

yet hanging in the stars . . . One of the touches of foreboding which appear from time to time; the events of the play are propelled by fate and Romeo's gloomy prophecy emphasizes this.

consequence . . . date . . . expire A legal metaphor which charts the action of the play.

Strike, drum The revellers are accompanied by a drummer-boy and Benvolio's instruction is that they shall continue on their way.

Act I Scene 5

The action at the start of this scene is clearly intended to follow directly after Scene 4; Romeo and Benvolio are already on stage for the start of the feast and the entry of Capulet and his guests. The appearance of the Servants gives a stir to the action when it is threatening to become too static; Capulet's energetic, slightly disjointed and faintly colloquial welcome shows a side of him that is different from any we have seen so far. He talks to his relatives of their youthful dancing days, but dramatically this is all intended to lead up to Romeo's first sight of Juliet. Romeo speaks of her in a series of new and vital images which centre round light – here of a torch burning in the darkness but later to lead into the characteristic features of the play which derive from the light issuing from the sun. Rosaline is immediately forgotten – she is never mentioned as appearing at the feast except by implication where Romeo confirms Benvolio's prediction of I.2.89. The meeting of Romeo and Juliet is delayed further by the interruption of the crudely violent Tybalt and his dismissal by an unusually benign but always authoritative Capulet.

Commentary

The first meeting of Romeo and Juliet which follows starts to establish what made the play an immediate success, a success which ensured that it has been read as well as acted ever since, and which ultimately derives from a sincerity and a depth that was new to the Elizabethan stage. The first words the two lovers exchange are in the form of a conventional sonnet. We have already seen one of these in the Prologue to Act I and they serve as a reminder that the success of *Romeo and Juliet* is firmly rooted in the achievements of Shakespeare's early maturity as well as those of his contemporaries, as any courtier unable to produce a competent sonnet about 1590 risked being ignored. The imagery of the sonnet turns from light to that of religion, but it is significant that during this moment of deep emotion both Romeo and Juliet use a good deal of word-play; Mercutio is by no means the only character to use a number of puns. The scene is concluded with Juliet anxiously inquiring the identity of her new admirer from the Nurse, and, with a touch of dramatic irony, recognizing that her love is fated, as Romeo has already done at I, 4, 107.

If the language that the two lovers use to one another has as yet no special distinction, it has already advanced a good deal on anything that either uses before they meet – Juliet's detached talk about Paris or Romeo's stylized moonings about Rosaline.

When . . . hands i.e. When only one or two men do their duty.

foul Punning on (1) shameful (2) dirty.

joint-stools Ordinary wooden stools.

court-cupboard Large cupboard for storing food; silver plate might be placed on it.

marchpane Marzipan.

the longer liver take all A proverb meaning enjoy life while you can.

makes dainty Demurely hesitates.

Am I come near ye now? Have I hit the real truth?

A hall Clear the hall!

turn the tables up i.e. take them off their trestles and stack them against the wall.

quench the fire . . . Shakespeare had forgotten that the play is set in July. The poem by Brooke that was his source set the story at Christmas.

unlook'd-for sport i.e. the party of Masquers.

Pentecost Whitsuntide.

a ward Under the control of a guardian before his twenty-first birthday.

Ethiop's Negro's; the word is chosen for its exotic quality.

use Everyday wear.

The measure done When the dance is over.

Forswear it Withdraw the oath sworn (to Rosaline).

antic face Mask.

solemnity Celebration.

Content thee Keep your temper.

disparagement Discourtesy.

ill-beseeming semblance Inappropriate outward appearance.

goodman boy My fine fellow – Capulet is deliberately patronizing.

set cock-a-hoop Set everything in confusion.

scathe Injure.

princox Presumptuous upstart.

Patience perforce Enforced patience.

choler Rage.

intrusion i.e. Romeo's.

If I profane . . . purged The length and elaboration of the comparison to religion (profane holy shrine, sin, pilgrims, devotion, saints, holy palmers, prayer, faith, trespass) is a good example of an Elizabethan conceit. It shows that both Romeo and Juliet are equally ingenious in statement and reply. The concluding couplet of the sonnet is sealed with the lovers' first kiss.

This holy shrine Juliet's hand.

wrong By calling it profane.

mannerly Modest and appropriate.

palm . . . palmer's A pun on (1) palm of the hand (2) palmer – a pilgrim who had returned from the holy land – originally carrying a palm.

faith i.e. *my* faith.
move Change from what they know to be right.
took Taken.
trespass sweetly urg'd Sin put forward attractively.
by th' book According to a set formula.
What is her mother? What is her position?
chinks Money.
O dear account A sad reckoning.
my foe's debt At the mercy of my family enemy.
the sport is at the best There is nothing better to come. Romeo then
  applies the remark to himself, a form of dramatic irony.
trifling foolish banquet towards A few things to eat on the way.
fay Faith.
waxes Grows.
yond gentleman The gentleman over there – because by pointing to
  two in which she has no interest, Juliet wishes to disguise the real
  object of her enquiry.
Too early . . . late I saw him too early without knowing who he was, and
  once I had known it was too late.
Prodigious birth i.e. The love I have given birth to is a monster.

Revision questions on Act I

1 Compare the use Shakespeare makes of the conversation of
servants in Scene 1 to that in Scene 5.
2 What is the attitude of (a) Capulet and (b) Lady Capulet to
their daughter's proposed marriage to Paris?
3 What do we find out in the course of the act about Romeo's
love for Rosaline?
4 Describe the first meeting of Romeo and Juliet.
5 What do we learn from this act of the character of Capulet?
6 What use does Shakespeare make of the Capulet feast and
how vividly does he portray it?
7 How much use does Shakespeare make of word-play in the
act?

Act II Prologue

We already know what the Prologue tells us; it does not comment on what we have seen and is little more than versified
narrative. As a result it is frequently omitted in performance.

old desire Romeo's love for Rosaline.
young affection His new-found love for Juliet.

gapes Eagerly awaits.
That fair i.e. Rosaline.
Alike Both equally.
foe i.e. because she is a Capulet.
suppos'd Thought by everyone else.
complain Make love-laments.
from fearful hooks i.e. at great risk.
use to Usually.
Tempering extremities Softening hardships.

Act II Scene 1

While returning from the feast Romeo gives Mercutio and Benvolio the slip in order to climb the wall into Capulet's garden; Mercutio uses the opportunity to make a series of bawdy jokes about Romeo's love, but soon gives up and goes home.

Commentary

This scene shows Mercutio once more as the prime mover; Benvolio has little to say. The mood is similar to that of the last scene, in which we saw them together, on the way to the Capulet feast. There, however, Romeo was present to act as something of a restraining influence on Mercutio; here, he is not, as far as they are aware. The result is that Mercutio is given speeches which are parodies of Elizabethan rhetoric: 'He heareth not, he stirreth not, he moveth not' but they are also exceedingly bawdy, perhaps less on superficial acquaintance than when one examines them closely. The dramatic reason for this is to set Mercutio's conception of love against the transformed and purified version experienced by Romeo which is to emerge so fully in the next scene.

dull earth i.e. his own body.
centre i.e. his spiritual core.
orchard garden (not necessarily containing fruit trees).
conjure ... Mercutio comically summons spirits by uttering parodies of magic words.
Ay me These were the words of Romeo's second speech in the play.
my gossip Venus My old friend Venus (the goddess of love).
purblind Totally blind (and therefore unable to see his target).
demesnes Territories, areas.
To raise ... down A series of very bawdy puns: **raise a spirit** (1) conjure up a demon (2) gain an erection ('spirit' is the Elizabethan

word for semen); **mistress' circle** (1) magic circle (2) vagina; **strange nature** belonging to someone else; **letting it there stand** (1) remain there (2) remain in sexual erection; **laid it and conjur'd it down** (1) made it powerless and banished it (2) caused the erection to subside.

raise up him (1) cause him to appear (2) give him an erection.

humorous Changeable, moody.

medlars A fruit supposed to resemble the female sexual organs. There is also a pun on 'meddler', which refers to sexual activity.

open-arse A dialect name for a medlar.

poperin pear Puns on (1) a pear which grew in Poperinghe (Flanders) (2) the literal 'pop her in' and (3) the shape of the glans penis.

truckle-bed A bed which could be pushed under another bed.

field-bed Camp-bed here meaning 'lying on the ground'. All this talk of beds is intended to be heard by Romeo and reflects the bantering talk of young men in company together.

Act II Scene 2

As Mercutio and Benvolio depart, Romeo comes out of hiding and sees Juliet at a window. Totally ignorant of his presence she starts to speak and reveals that she is as obsessed with the thought of Romeo as he is with her. Romeo then reveals himself; at first she is frightened and then embarrassed that he has heard so frank a confession of her true feelings. They exchange 'love's faithful vow' and express their intention of getting married as soon as possible.

Commentary

This is one of the most memorable scenes in the play. It uses that most flexible feature of the Elizabethan stage, the balcony, to notable effect; it is full of effectively used light imagery to contrast with the darkness against which the scene is set and the ever-present threat of discovery by the Capulets before the affair has had a chance to develop. The other effectively used contrast is that between the bawdy adolescent humour of the newly-departed Mercutio and Romeo's painfully felt sincerity.

He ... wound The rhyme with the last line of the previous scene shows that the scene division is artificial and that the action follows straight on.

Be not her maid i.e. do not be a servant to Diana, goddess of the moon and also of chastity; do not live unmarried.

vestal livery Maidenly uniform (the priestesses of Vesta vowed a life of chastity).

sick and green Shakespeare is probably thinking of the green sickness, a form of anaemia often fatal to young women in his time.

fools Perhaps referring to the motley colours in a fool's uniform.

discourses Speaks the language of love.

wherefore art thou Why is your name Romeo? (a member of the Montague family.)

though not a Montague Even if you were not a Montague i.e. whatever name you go by.

owes Possesses.

counsel Private thoughts.

By a name . . . who I am I do not know which name to use to tell you who I am.

o'erperch Fly over.

but thou love me If you do not love me.

prorogued Postponed.

wanting of Without.

I lent him eyes Remember that Cupid is blind (see II, 1, 12 also).

Else . . . cheek . . . The maiden blush is an indication of modesty, and one which Juliet displays on several occasions. (See II, 5, 71; III, 2, 14.)

fain Willingly.

dwell on form Preserve correct behaviour.

compliment Formality.

fond Foolish.

cunning to be strange Skill in seeming aloof.

discovered Revealed.

changes in her circled orb Waxes and wanes in her path across the sky.

contract Exchange of vows of betrothal.

frank (1) generous (2) open.

thy bent of love The aim of your love.

procure Arrange.

strife Efforts.

So thrive my soul May my soul prosper (a mild oath).

Hist! Listen!

tassel-gentle A male falcon (this and 'lure' are images from falconry, where the falcon is attracted back to the falconer).

Bondage is hoarse i.e. because my parents are very strict I must whisper.

Else . . . name The reference is to a story from Greek mythology. The nymph Echo, pining for her love Narcissus (who is indifferent to her) wastes away and ultimately becomes no more than a voice, living only in caves. Juliet is saying that she would outdo Echo.

attending Listening.

My nyas A young hawk which has not yet left the nest.

still Constantly.

wanton's bird The pet of an irresponsible girl who teases her pets.

gyves Fetters.
So loving-jealous of his liberty So fond of the bird that she is jealous of its regaining its liberty.
so sweet i.e. in such sweet places.
fleckled Dappled.
Titan's wheels In classical mythology the sun god, Phoebus, drove a chariot across the sky.
ghostly Spiritual father i.e. a priest.
dear hap Good fortune.

Act II Scene 3

Friar Laurence is introduced gathering the herbs which he uses for medical purposes; and this interest in herbs prepares us for the profound influence he will have on the later action of the play. Romeo enters and asks him to consent to marrying him that day. The Friar at first supposes that Rosaline is still the object of his affections but on learning that these have now been transferred to Juliet, the Friar agrees to perform the marriage in the hope that it will bury the feud between the two families.

Commentary

The scene carries the action forward swiftly and shows the Friar as good-humoured, a little patronizing and well-intentioned; but little aware, by the readiness with which he consents to the proposed marriage, of the problems that it will raise and having an over-sanguine confidence in his ability to solve them.

advance Rises higher in the sky.
osier cage Willow basket.
ours The friar belonged to a brotherhood.
baleful Harmful.
precious-juiced Having wonderful properties in their juices.
The earth ... tomb i.e. all life springs from the earth and when dead returns to it. The next three lines repeat the idea, comparing the earth to a mother.
mickle Great.
stones Rocks and minerals.
strain'd Perverted.
Revolts from true birth Because it is aware of the creative purpose for which it was intended, it refuses to co-operate when it is misused.
by action dignified Becomes virtuous when it is used for a noble purpose.

infant rind Seedling stalk.

that part Its scent.

with the heart By stopping the heart.

still Always.

rude will Earthy desire.

the worser is predominant i.e. rude will has more influence.

canker The canker-worm or caterpillar.

Benedicite May God bless you!

distemper'd Unbalanced, upset.

keeps his watch i.e. is ever present.

unbruisèd . . . brain Youth as yet unaffected by the world with a brain free from anxiety.

distemperature Mental disturbance.

mine enemy i.e. the Capulets.

Both our remedies The remedy for both of us.

steads my foe Helps my enemy (Juliet).

shrift Absolution.

all combin'd Everything agreed.

as we pass As we walk along.

Holy Saint Francis! The patron saint of his order (the Franciscans).

sentence Proverb.

Women may i.e. no wonder that women fall.

Thy love . . . spell Your love was like a child who has learned something by heart without understanding what has been learned.

In one respect On account of one thing.

stand on Am anxious for.

Act II Scene 4

Benvolio and Mercutio later that morning lament the loss of Romeo to love and, as they think, Rosaline. They know that he has not been home that night and that Tybalt has sent him a challenge as the result of his appearance at the Capulets' feast. Romeo then arrives and proves himself such a match for Mercutio's witticisms that they consider him restored to the person they knew before he fell in love. At the Nurse's entry, indeed, Romeo takes his friends' part before they leave him to talk with her alone. She is anxious that Romeo may be trying to take advantage of her young mistress' innocence, but he tells her to convey a message to Juliet that she must make an excuse to go to confession at Friar Laurence's cell that same afternoon; there they will be married.

Commentary

The scene is largely a comic one. For the first part the comedy is a continuation of the word-play that we have seen from Mercutio in earlier scenes; and as the main dramatic purpose of Mercutio and the Nurse is to act as foils to Romeo and Juliet it is interesting to see them together – the only time throughout the play when they meet. They are both bawdy but Mercutio's bawdiness is a good deal more subtle than the Nurse's. Here she is quite unable to see the funny side of a situation and she proves notably sharp with her servant Peter when, in her opinion, he fails to defend her adequately.

tonight Last night.
answer it (1) respond to it (Benvolio) (2) reply (Mercutio).
dared Challenged.
pin The centre of the target in archery.
blind bow-boy's Cupid's.
butt-shaft Arrow used in shooting practice (at the butts).
Prince of Cats A pun on Tybalt's name as it appears in the story of 'Reynard the Fox'. The cat's name there is Tybert.
prick-song Music written out by hand or printed; i.e. accurately.
proportion Balance.
minim rests This continues the musical metaphor and means that Tybalt will feint twice before hitting the target.
butcher of a silk button An allusion to Tybalt's accuracy in fencing.
first and second cause Knowledge of the rules of duelling; there were two principal causes of duels – crimes punishable by death and matters of honour.
immortal passado . . . punto reverso . . . hay Fencing terms of Italian origin meaning a step forward, a back-handed stroke, and the final thrust, from the cry of the duellist as he made it, meaning (in Italian) 'you have it'. The play contains many references to fencing.
of To.
new tuners of accents Speakers in the latest fashion, who affect all the new idioms and mannerisms of speech.
By Jesu . . . whore! Mercutio proceeds to imitate the language of the people he has just been talking about.
grandsire This is mockingly addressed to Benvolio.
strange flies Those who buzz about and waste their energy.
fashion-mongers Those concerned only with fashion.
pardon-me's Those who are affected in their speech.
stand . . . on Insist on.
their bones Their over-sensitive bodies.
without his roe Punning on Romeo's name (1) *Ro*meo (2) roe – sperm of male fish possibly (3) *Ro*saline.

fishified Made like a fish; made bloodless.

numbers Lines of poetry. The Italian poet Petrarch composed numerous sonnets to his love Laura.

to his lady Compared with his lady.

There follows a list of several of the great lovers of history, included to show what to Mercutio is the strength of Romeo's infatuation, as all these are trivial compared with his (as Mercutio supposes) Rosaline.

Dido Queen of Carthage, who after a passionate affair with Aeneas, was deserted by him when he departed to found Rome, and killed herself.

dowdy A slut.

Cleopatra Queen of Egypt (hence 'gypsy') whose passionate love affair with Mark Antony resulted in their suicides.

Helen Wife of Menelaus, King of Sparta and the most beautiful woman in the world who was abducted by Paris and taken to Troy; this was the cause of the Trojan war.

Hero Of Sestos, whose love Leander swam across the Dardanelles nightly to see her.

hildings Much the same as 'harlots'.

Thisbe Whose love affair with Pyramus was conducted through the crack in the party wall separating their houses and in the teeth of parental opposition.

French slop Baggy trousers as worn in France at the time.

The slip Explains Mercutio's pun to Romeo. As well as meaning 'you escaped from us' it was a slang word for a counterfeit coin.

conceive Understand.

courtesy There now starts a series of puns on courtesy – curtsy – courteous which leads to the 'pink of courtesy'. The 'pink' is the highest degree of courtesy and provides the starting-point for the next display of wit. 'Pink' is a flower and Romeo's shoes ('pumps') are decorated with leather punched in patterns ('pinked'). Romeo has to follow Mercutio and will therefore wear out his shoes' **sole**; 'solely' also means 'only'.

singular (1) unique (2) single, on its own.

single-soled ... singleness Threadbare joke only remarkable for its feebleness.

Come between ... faints Mercutio ironically appeals to Benvolio to come between then as he cannot keep up with the pace of this verbal fencing-match; in so doing he unconsciously prefigures what is going to happen in the duel with Tybalt.

Switch and spurs A metaphor from horse-racing i.e. urge your wits to go faster!

a match Claim that I have won.

wild-goose chase i.e. my following you. A wild-goose chase involved two riders who started together and as soon as one obtained the lead the other had to follow him.

wild-goose Fool.

Was I . . . goose? Did I keep up with you?

bite thee by the ear A term of affection; their war is a friendly one.

sweeting A sweet apple; usually served as a sauce with goose.

cheveril A flexible leather made out of the skin of a kid.

an ell 45 inches or 1m 12cm.

broad (1) wide (2) bawdy (3) obvious.

by art By skill.

natural Idiot.

bauble (1) the fool's sign of his position, a stick with a fool's head as mascot on top (2) penis.

tale (1) story (2) penis.

against the hair (1) against the grain, when it should have continued (2) up against the pubic hair.

tale large (1) lengthy (2) an erection.

occupy the argument 'Occupy' was an indecent word in Elizabethan times; this makes it plain that Mercutio's bawdy remark has two clear senses.

goodly gear Said in reference to the Nurse who, as she comes, looks like a bundle of clothes.

A sail This is Mercutio's comment on her appearance.

A shirt and smock A man and a woman.

for fault of a worse In default. Romeo humorously reverses the usual proverb 'in default of a better'.

confidence A malapropism for 'conference'.

endite Invite; a further (deliberate) malapropism.

A bawd Mercutio chooses to imagine that the Nurse runs a brothel.

So ho. This is the cry made when hunting the hare and a hare is sighted. Mercutio's jokes are about hares, which he punningly confuses with whores.

a lenten pie A poor sort of pie using bad meat.

stale (1) dry and old (2) a prostitute.

hoar (1) grey-haired (2) whore.

spent Used up.

Farewell . . . lady This is the refrain of an old ballad.

saucy merchant Impudent fellow.

ropery Indecent jesting.

stand to Stand by.

take him down Humiliate him.

jacks Low fellows.

flirt-gills Loose women.

skains-mates Cut-throats.

use you at his pleasure Peter picks up the bawdy aspect of this unintentionally bawdy remark from the Nurse; his 'weapon' is (1) his sword and (2) his penis.

in Into.

a fool's paradise i.e. merely intend to seduce her.

weak dealing Contemptible behaviour.

protest In its colloquial sense this meant 'I swear love'. The Nurse thinks Romeo is making her an offer.

shriv'd This is the verb from 'shrift' i.e. absolved.

cords . . . stair A rope ladder.

quit Reward.

lay knife aboard Lay claim to her.

as lief She would rather.

I anger her . . . properer man An attempt by Shakespeare to make it appear that the affair between Romeo and Juliet has lasted for longer than the one day it seems to have occupied so far.

clout in the versal world Piece of cloth in the (uni)versal world.

rosemary The flower used as a symbol of remembrance and therefore used at weddings and funerals.

the dog's name, 'R' So called because a rolled R resembles the growling of a dog; her mentioning this is an indication of the Nurse's butterfly mind.

sententious Malapropism for 'sentences', that is, proverbs.

Before, and apace Go in front of me, and quickly.

Act II Scene 5

Juliet is impatiently waiting for the return of the Nurse from her meeting with Romeo. When the Nurse eventually arrives it takes Juliet some time to wring this essential information out of her.

Commentary

Dramatically the scene emphasizes Juliet's desperate anxiety that her affair should progress, her powerlessness to do anything about it unaided, and further develops aspects of the Nurse's character.

Therefore . . . doves i.e. that is why nimble-winged doves draw Venus in her chariot.

highmost hill The zenith or highest point of his journey.

bandy her Hit her (a metaphor from tennis, continued from 'ball' in the previous line).

many feign as they Many behave as if they.

give me leave Leave me alone.

jaunce Jaunt.

I'll stay the circumstance I'll wait for all the details.

simple Foolish.

not to be talked on (1) not worth talking about (2) discussion of him is forbidden.

compare Comparison.

Go thy ways That's enough!
Beshrew Curse.
Where should she be? Where do you expect her to be?
hot Passionate.
Marry, come up, I trow A colloquial expression of impatience.
coil Fuss.
hie you Hasten.
They'll ... news Any news immediately makes you blush.
you ... night (1) you shall have to bear the responsibility at night (2) you will have to bear the weight of your lover at night.

Act II Scene 6

Friar Laurence and Romeo await the arrival of the bride; as she has been on stage at the end of the previous scene their conversation continues for fifteen lines before her arrival. When Juliet does arrive it is with great urgency as the original stage direction tells us. The Friar marries them.

Commentary

This scene is short and functional.

close Unite.
do May do.
triumph Consummation, flash-point.
fire and powder Gunpowder.
loathsome ... deliciousness i.e. it is so sweet that it becomes cloying and sickly.
confounds Destroys.
gossamers Threads of a spider's web.
wanton Playful.
ghostly Spiritual.
Romeo ... both The Friar is unable to kiss Juliet so asks Romeo to undertake the task for him.
As ... much Juliet wishes the kisses to be returned as she cannot accept them without returning them.
blazon An image from heraldry, meaning to describe its various colours and form.
sweeten ... air Sweeten the air with the sound of your voice.
Conceit ... matter Fancy richer in content.
I ... wealth i.e. I am unable to count even half the sum that I possess.

Revision questions on Act II

1 Describe the meeting between Romeo and Juliet. Why is it likely to be effective on the stage?
2 What does Scene 3 tells us about the Friar?
3 Compare Mercutio's speeches in Scene 2 with that delivered by Romeo before he reveals himself to Juliet in Scene 2.
4 What do Benvolio, Mercutio and Romeo talk about before the arrival of the Nurse in Scene 4?
5 How is the Nurse's character developed in Scenes 4 and 5?
6 Why is the marriage scene so short? Does it contain anything of interest apart from carrying the story forward?
7 Why does the Nurse speak partly in verse and partly in prose in Scene 5?

Act III Scene 1

Benvolio and Mercutio are jesting in their usual manner when they meet Tybalt and the Capulets; Mercutio's banter rouses Tybalt to anger and then Romeo arrives to be taunted for his presence at the Capulet feast. Romeo is conciliatory to a man who is now his relation by marriage, but to Mercutio this is 'dishonourable vile submission' – an insult not to be borne. A fight soon develops and Romeo, in trying to prevent it, causes Mercutio to be gravely wounded; his last word characteristically is a pun as he is carried off. His death, which immediately follows, spurs Romeo to gain revenge, and in the ensuing fight Tybalt too is killed. This revival of the inter-family brawl once more brings the Prince to the scene and he banishes Romeo for his part in it.

Commentary

Mercutio's departure from the plot is dramatically necessary because his lively personality is threatening to eclipse that of Romeo. The action has been preoccupied with the love-affair of Romeo and Juliet for most of the last act; now the politics and feuds of Verona so vividly described in Act I reappear to provide another tension to menace their marriage. The scene is also effective in that it immediately follows one full of emotion of a very different sort.

operation The effects of the alcohol.

drawer The waiter (who draws the liquor from the casks).

hot a Jack Quick-tempered a fellow.

moved to be moody Inclined to be ill-tempered.

moody to be moved Ill-tempered at being provoked.

What eye . . . ? Mercutio is punning on Benvolio's 'I' in line 10 but attributing to him faults which are more evident in himself.

meat Food, not necessarily flesh.

doublet The Elizabethan equivalent of a jacket.

before Easter Then, as now, new fashions came out at Easter, and this tailor would be attempting to make money by anticipating them.

fee simple of my life Absolute title to ownership of my life.

for an hour and a quarter Implying that at the end of that time he would be dead – an example of dramatic irony.

O simple! O simpleton!

Could you . . . giving Punning on 'giving' and 'taking'.

thou consortest with You keep company with. The use of 'thou' indicates that the degree of contempt he is using has increased sharply.

Consort? The regular word for a group of musicians; hired ones were considered inferior.

fiddlestick Sword.

Zounds An oath, short for 'God's wounds' (those received by Christ on the Cross).

coldly Coolly, calmly.

my man The man I am looking for.

wear your livery Mercutio persists in purposely misunderstanding Tybalt. 'My man' he takes to mean 'my servant'; servants normally wore a uniform.

he'll be your follower (1) your servant (2) he will be keen to fight a duel.

field A place where they might fight a duel.

villain A deep insult on Romeo with regard to (1) his birth (2) his behaviour.

Doth . . . greeting Largely excuses the rage I would normally display on being greeted in such a manner.

knowest me not Do not know my feelings towards you.

Boy Here a term of contempt (as it is when used by Capulet in I,5).

injuries Insults.

devise Imagine.

Till . . . love Until the marriage is brought into the open.

tender Hold, value.

Alla stoccata A thrust with the rapier. Mercutio is referring to Tybalt's style of fighting, and therefore to Tybalt himself. The line therefore means 'Rapier-man is saying something like that and getting away with it!'.

rat-catcher Mercutio has called him the 'King of Cats' in II,4,19.

walk i.e. to a quiet place where we can fight a duel.

That . . . eight i.e. I mean to have one of them and depending on the way you behave afterwards beat the remaining eight (without drawing blood).

pilcher Scabbard.

ears Hilt.

sped Finished with.

and hath nothing Unhurt.

a scratch Still punning on Tybalt's role as 'King of Cats'.

villain Here not used insultingly – merely to a servant.

a grave man It is entirely characteristic of Mercutio that he puns in what is almost his last breath.

by the book of arithmetic According to a set plan laid down in the fencing manuals. Mercutio has previously said that in his fighting Tybalt 'keeps time distance and proportion'.

ally Relative.

very True.

temper (1) mood (2) tempering (as of steel).

aspired Risen to.

on mo days doth depend Hangs over the future.

respective lenity Respectful gentleness.

conduct Guiding principle.

This shall determine that i.e. his sword will decide that.

doom thee death Sentence you to death.

fortune's fool The sport of fortune, its helpless victim.

Up, sir, go with me Though this line is given to a 'Citizen' he is clearly a man of authority.

discover Reveal.

manage Course.

my cousin Much vaguer in Elizabethan times than now – it refers to any relative.

true Just.

nice Trivial.

withal In addition.

Could . . . spleen Could not persuade the ill-tempered Tybalt to peace. Benvolio omits to say that Mercutio first provoked Tybalt.

tilts Makes a lunge at.

as hot i.e. hot-tempered.

Cold death i.e. Tybalt's sword.

Retorts it Turns it back. The indications are that Mercutio and Tybalt fought with weapons in each hand – rapier and dagger.

envious Malicious.

Who . . . revenge Who had only just thought of taking his revenge.

Who . . . owe? Who now is to pay for his death with his own life?

His fault . . . end i.e. he has only taken the law into his own hands.

we The Prince is here speaking in his official capacity and uses the royal 'we'. In the next line he is speaking as a private person and uses 'I'.

interest i.e. personal interest.
your hearts' proceeding Action proceeding from your hearts' anger.
My blood Mercutio was the Prince's relation.
amerce you Punish you.
the loss of mine My loss.
purchase out Make amends for.
Bear hence this body Tybalt's body has been on stage since his death
   and is a visible reminder of the violence that has occurred. The open
   Elizabethan stage made it necessary to carry it off to prepare for the
   next scene.
Mercy . . . kill Giving pardon to murderers only causes more murders
   to take place.

Act III Scene 2

Juliet is longing for darkness as she waits impatiently for Romeo
on her wedding-night. The nurse's entry abruptly changes the
mood; as in Act II Scene 5, she is slow to come to the point and
Juliet's reaction is a confused one until the Nurse directly attacks
her husband. At this she leaps to his defence, and is quick to
realize that Romeo has narrowly escaped death at the hands of
her cousin. When she hears that Romeo is at Friar Laurence's
cell, she asks the Nurse to take a ring to him before he comes to
take his last farwewell.

Commentary

The most subtle feature of this scene is Juliet's first speech. It is
expressed in language that is at once formal, imaginative, and
subtly erotic. It starts with classical imagery, but soon changes to
what is almost a prayer that shows Juliet anxious to lose her
virginity and longing for union with Romeo in ways that
emphasize the physical quite as much as they emphasize the
spiritual. The speech is also extremely dramatic in that the
audience knows that Juliet's ecstasy is likely to be short-lived
because she does not yet know of the events of the previous
scene. After the Nurse's entry the scene loses its power somewhat, as Juliet's puns seem forced and her oxymorons equally
contrived; it regains something of that power in her spirited
defence of Romeo.

you fiery-footed steeds i.e. those that drew the chariot of the sun-god
   across the sky.

Phoebus' lodging The destination of the sun-god below the western horizon.

Phaeton Son of the sun-god, he was allowed to take charge of the chariot for one day, but drove so wildly that the horses rushed out of their usual track and came too near the earth. To save the earth from getting scorched Jupiter, king of the gods, killed him by throwing a thunderbolt. The ironic comparison with Romeo's and Juliet's own story is evident.

love-performing i.e. making it easy for lovers.

runaway's eyes may wink No one knows what this really means; it is suspected that the text here is faulty. The general sense seems to be that the eyes of people who might see Romeo should be closed.

civil Grave, serious.

lose a winning match Win her beloved by surrendering to him.

Hood my unmann'd blood . . . cheeks These are all metaphors from falconry.

unmann'd An untamed hawk (but also Juliet has no experience of a man).

bating Refers to the fact that the hawk would flutter on the wrist in agitation unless it was hooded. Juliet has already confessed her tendency to blush easily.

till strange . . . modesty Till my reserve is broken down and thinks the actions of true love a very ordinary thing.

when I shall die . . . This is at once a premonition of the lovers' fate – to be united in death, and a pun on the peak of sexual ecstasy which Juliet is so looking forward to.

garish Gaudy, glaring.

weraday Similar to alas!

envious Full of malice.

Romeo can The Nurse's meaning is that it is malicious of Romeo to have killed Tybalt, though Juliet does not of course yet know this.

Say thou but 'Ay' . . . or if not, 'No' Juliet's puns on 'I', 'Ay' and 'Eye' were long thought to be most inappropriate at such a time. They are characteristic of Shakespeare at the period when he wrote this play, and audiences then would no doubt have thought them both subtle and ingenious.

cockatrice A fabulous beast reputed to be able to kill with a look.

those eyes i.e. Romeo's eyes.

Brief sounds . . . weal or woe Let brief sounds decide whether or not I will be happy. The 'brief sounds' are 'ay' or 'no'.

God save the mark A proverb, used in the context of any misfortune; here the Nurse is perhaps pointing at her own breast to show where the mark was.

corse Corpse – though its meaning was less harsh than the modern word.

gore-blood Clotted blood.

swounded Fainted.

bankrupt i.e. as it had lost all it possessed.

To prison, eyes i.e. may you be shut for ever.

Vile earth Addressing her own body ('Dust thou art and unto dust shalt thou return' Genesis iii,20).

one heavy bier i.e. because it carried the weight of two bodies.

honest Honourable. The Nurse's description reveals a Tybalt somewhat different from the one we have seen on stage.

so contrary In opposite directions.

the general doom i.e. for the world's Day of Judgment.

show Appearance.

Just Exact.

justly Rightly – another play on words.

hadst thou to do Were you about.

bower Embower, enclose.

book ... bound A metaphor previously used in Lady Capulet's speech in I,3.

naught Worthless, wicked.

where's my man? It is ironic that immediately after having condemned all men the Nurse asks for her own 'man' (servant).

aqua vitae Brandy.

speak well ... speak ill ... This passage uses a good deal of antithesis like this; note also smooth/mangled; villain/villain cousin.

forget it fain Willingly forget it.

Hath slain i.e. on balance is equal, to the death of.

And needly ... griefs Will inevitably be followed by other griefs.

Thy father ... mother My father or my mother. She is talking to herself.

Which modern ... mov'd Which more everyday lamentation might have prompted.

rearward Piece of news tacked on to the end. A metaphor from the rearguard of an army.

that word's death i.e. the death involved in the word 'banished'.

sound (1) express (2) plumb (as in finding the depth of water under a ship).

beguil'd Cheated (of your purpose).

wot Know.

Act III Scene 3

Romeo is at the Friar's cell and hears the Prince's sentence of banishment with a despair that threatens to become a frenzy. The Friar is about to advise him when the Nurse arrives with news that Juliet's reaction to the event is similar to Romeo's. The advice he proceeds to give is extremely practical; after his wedding-night Romeo is to flee to the neighbouring town of Mantua, there to await the repeal of the banishment and his own recall. The Nurse prepares to give Juliet the message and produces the ring which does much to reassure Romeo that his wife still wants him.

Commentary

The effect of Romeo's reaction is to emphasize his youth and naivety, contrasted with the Friar's maturity. Some dramatic tension is inserted into the scene with the arrival of the Nurse; we do not know who it is that is knocking at the door, and fear that Romeo may be discovered by the authorities before he has obeyed the letter of the Prince's command. The preparations for the consummation of the marriage could hardly come at a worse time.

Affliction ... calamity Word-play afflicts the Friar as it does everyone else in this play. Here it comes from love (enamour'd ... wedded). There is also in the background the constantly repeated idea that both of the lovers are marrying death.

parts Good qualities.

doom Judgement.

Too familiar ... company i.e. you are too used to living with bad news. He implies that the news he brings now is good news.

vanish'd A curious word to use; the sense seems to be 'came gently from his lips' but there may be an error in printing or transcription.

without Outside.

banished Romeo's obsessive repetition of the word recalls Juliet's in the last scene.

with a golden axe i.e. you call it by a more attractive name but the effect is just as deadly.

rush'd aside The word contains the idea of quickly and arbitrarily pushing aside.

validity Value.

mean (1) device (2) contemptible.

fond Foolish.

Hang up i.e. get rid of.

Displant Transplant.

dispute Talk (it over).

Thou canst ... not feel Romeo is saying that the Friar as a celibate can have no idea of what love is really like.

Taking ... grave He lies on the ground inert as if to show how large a grave should be dug for him.

infold me Protect me. At this point the Friar is addressing the unknown visitor and Romeo alternately.

simpleness Foolishness – referring to Romeo's tantrums.

woeful sympathy An agreement to be miserable.

For Juliet's sake ... Deep an O. Another example of the Nurse's tendency to speak bawdily (sometimes at a most inappropriate time) through long practice.

deadly level of a gun A gun pointed with deadly aim.

anatomy i.e. his own body.

And ill-beseeming ... both And an unnatural beast in appearing to be both (an ill-behaved woman with the appearance of a man).

damned Suicide was a mortal sin.

usurer The money-lenders of Elizabethan society were rarely popular. Shakespeare's usual idea is that of the parable of the talents – that it is sinful to hoard. 'Use' means lending out money at interest, and here is one of three words played on; usurer, usest, use.

Killing If it kills.

Thy wit ... both i.e. Your intelligence – that quality which is complementary to good looks and affection – is being ill-directed in the pursuit of either.

powder i.e. gunpowder; soldiers carried their powder in 'flasks'.

dismember'd ... defence Blown to pieces by your own weapon.

dead i.e. ready to die.

Thou ... fortune Thou poutest on thy good fortune.

Ascend It had been arranged that Romeo would climb to Juliet's room by rope ladder.

the Watch be set At nightfall the City gates would be closed and the guard would start patrolling.

blaze Announce publicly.

Which heavy sorrow ... unto Which deep mourning makes them more likely to do.

here stands all your state I will summarize your position.

Every good hap Everything favourable.

so brief to part i.e. to part with so few words.

Act III Scene 4

Paris's request to marry Juliet, last heard of in Act I Scene 2, is revived at a time when both Romeo and Juliet are deeply distressed and the joy of their first meetings has been threatened by the pressure of outside events.

Commentary

This development provides a further threatening factor and Capulet's steely determination to proceed with the match prepares us for his unsympathetic reaction to Juliet's objections in the next scene.

move Persuade.

These times ... woo Paris here shows himself as able to play on words as any other character in the play; he also shows himself a gentleman by immediately preparing to leave on learning of Capulet's desire to go to bed.

mew'd up to her heaviness Caged up in her grief. Another metaphor from falconry; a hawk was put in a mew when she cast her feathers.

desperate tender Venturesome offer; 'desperate' because he has not yet obtained Juliet's consent, though to the audience the offer is desperate because we know that there is no chance that it will succeed.

ere you go to bed The hour, we have been told, is very late; it is surprising that Capulet should tell his wife to see Juliet in the middle of the night – but as the audience knows that she is spending the night with her husband it is dramatically very effective.

son Paris' It is plain that Capulet is conforming to the custom of the time and calling his future son-in-law 'son' before marriage.

Monday! Ha ha! The repetition of the various days of the week gives a new and added urgency to the situation. 'Ha ha!' expresses hesitation.

She shall be married His earlier suggestion has now become a command.

so late So recently.

carelessly Without regard.

against In readiness for.

Afore me A mild oath short for 'As God is before me'.

Act III Scene 5

Romeo and Juliet are about to bid each other farewell after their first and only night together before Romeo goes into banishment at Mantua. The Nurse arrives in haste to tell Juliet that her mother is coming, and Romeo drops from her balcony to the ground. Lady Capulet arrives with the news that Juliet is to be married to Paris within two days. She finds her daughter weeping and believes it to be for Tybalt. She promises revenge on Romeo, only to be answered in ambiguities that the audience under-stands, but which Lady Capulet does not. Juliet greets the news with horror and refuses indignantly. Capulet then enters as the affectionate father; on learning of Juliet's opposition to his plan he turns immediately into a tyrant, determined to inflict his will upon her. He abuses the Nurse savagely when she takes her young mistress's part, and the Nurse, unable to cope with the complexities of the situation, advises Juliet to commit bigamy and marry Paris. Juliet is left totally alone, and resolves to commit suicide rather than submit to the dictates of her father.

Commentary

This lengthy scene has material in it of the utmost contrast. It starts lyrically in what is almost a continuation of the earlier balcony scene both in setting and in imagery – one notices the characteristic light imagery reappearing. The position of the lovers quickly reverses, as at first it is Romeo who wishes to go and Juliet who wants him to stay; very soon she urges *him* to go with a sudden, energetic image:

It is the lark that sings so out of tune,
Straining harsh discords and unpleasing sharps.

The Gothic element which becomes more frequent in the latter part of the play first appears here:

Methinks I see thee, now thou art so low,
As one dead in the bottom of a tomb.

It also provides one of the main touches of dramatic irony for when Juliet next sees her husband he is indeed pale in the tomb. There then follows the conversation between mother and daughter where, with further dramatic irony, the audience and Juliet are party to double meanings which Lady Capulet cannot comprehend. The scene is also notable for the development in the character of Capulet who turns from a patronizing father to an objectionable boor within twenty lines. Lastly, the shallowness of the Nurse is for the first time fully revealed and at the end of the scene Juliet is totally alone with no one in whom she can confide.

fearful Sounds make him fearful because he dreads discovery by day.
lace the severing clouds Make holes in the clouds in the manner of lace.
Night's candles i.e. the stars.
meteor that the sun exhales Meteors were thought to be caused by the rays of the sun igniting vapours drawn up ('exhaled') from the earth by the sun's warmth. They were also bad omens.
so If.
reflex of Cynthia's brow A reflection of the Moon-goddess' forehead.
Nor that is not the lark This is a double negative used for emphasis.
division A trilling sound or rapid and separated notes; there is an obvious pun on 'divideth', meaning 'separates'.
the lark . . . change eyes A rustic fancy because the toad's eyes are beautiful and the lark's small and unattractive.

I would . . . too Because the toad's croak would be no 'herald of the morn'.

affray Frighten us (from each other's arms).

hunt's-up A morning song or greeting. The name was derived from the huntsman's early-morning song.

ill-divining soul A soul that foresees evil.

Dry sorrow drinks our blood Another old belief, that sorrow caused people to go pale through lack of blood.

down i.e. gone to bed – to lie down.

procures her Causes her to come.

how now What's the matter?

feeling loss Deeply-felt loss.

but not . . . weep for You will not feel the person of the friend you are lamenting.

Shall . . . dram Who will give him a dose (of poison) to which he is unaccustomed.

dead (1) his dead body (2) my poor heart is dead. There is yet another meaning, as next time Juliet sees Romeo, he *is* dead.

temper (1) mix the ingredients (2) nullify the effect of it.

wreak Repay.

needy i.e. when good news is scarce.

careful Caring.

in happy time What good luck (said sarcastically).

County see note p.23.

Here comes your father It is notable that Lady Capulet for the most part addresses her daughter as 'thou' whereas Juliet addresses her mother by the more formal 'you'. But to show her displeasure with Juliet Lady Capulet reverts to 'you' here.

It rains downright Remember that Juliet is weeping.

a conduit A spout with constant running water set in the street for communal use.

decree Decision – or perhaps even edict.

she will none . . . thanks She declines with thanks.

I would . . . grave Lady Capulet's curse comes true – further dramatic irony.

Take me with you Let me understand you.

proud i.e. that we have arranged such a marriage.

thankful that you have i.e. that you have done it out of love for me.

meant love Meant to be love – done with a loving motive.

Chopp'd logic Talking in riddles.

minion A spoilt child.

Thanks . . . prouds i.e. do not argue with me.

fettle Get ready.

hurdle A wooden framework on which prisoners were taken to punishment.

green-sickness Immature, unable to discriminate. 'Tallow-face' is much the same.

itch i.e. to hit you.

hilding A low, mean woman.

rate her Scold her.

Smatter Chatter.

O God'i'goode'en Goodbye, clear off!

hot Hot-tempered.

God's bread The Holy Sacrament.

still Always.

nobly lign'd Well-connected.

honourable parts Admirable personal qualities.

puling Whining.

mammet, in her fortune's tender A puppet who has had the fortune to have a good offer.

Graze i.e. feed.

Advise Think about it!

be forsworn Go back on my word.

I'll not speak a word i.e. in your favour.

How . . . earth? By what means can my vows of marriage be revoked except by the death of my husband?

practise stratagems Plot.

all the world to nothing The odds are very high.

challenge Claim.

beshrew Cursed be.

As living here . . . him As your living here and being unable to make any use of him.

Amen Juliet wishes that the Nurse's heart be cursed for giving her such unpalatable advice.

Well . . . much Juliet sees that she can expect no comfort from the Nurse, and her answer is deliberately ironic. It also means that she is quite alone and thrown completely on her own resources.

Ancient damnation! Wicked old woman!

forsworn To have gone back on my marriage vows.

Thou . . . twain i.e. I shall not come to you, for advice any more; our ways now must part.

Revision questions on Act III

1 Describe how (a) Mercutio and (b) Tybalt met their deaths.

2 Describe Juliet's reaction to the news of her cousin's death.

3 How does Romeo behave when he is in the Friar's cell? Do you approve of his behaviour?

4 Compare Capulet's treatment of Juliet after she has shown that she does not wish to marry Paris with his behaviour earlier in Act I.

5 In what ways does Romeo's and Juliet's last meeting in Scene 5 differ from their earlier one in Act II Scene 2?

6 Compare Lady Capulet's reaction to Juliet's predicament in Scene 5 to the Nurse's. What is the effect of both of them on Juliet?

Act IV Scene 1

Paris is visiting Friar Laurence to make arrangements for his planned marriage. The unenthusiastic Friar is soon joined by a more unenthusiastic Juliet; Paris greets her kindly, but Juliet can only convey her feelings by means of word-play whose ambiguities can readily be understood by the Friar and by the audience. As the occasion of Juliet's visit is ostensibly to come to confession, Paris tactfully leaves and Juliet is able to commune with the Friar in her grief. She tells him she would rather die than marry Paris. The Friar then puts forward his plan to administer a potion which will give Juliet the appearance of death for forty-two hours. She will awake in the Capulets' vault to be greeted by himself and the forewarned Romeo; the lovers will then make their escape to Mantua.

Commentary

After the succession of ambiguous answers given by Juliet to her mother in the previous scene, Act IV starts with her having to talk to Paris in a very similar way. In a play where word-play is so important, one can distinguish here a type that is peculiarly suited to Juliet – one that is evasive while retaining the modesty that is such an essential part of her character:

Paris Thy face is mine, and thou hast slander'd it.
Juliet It may be so for it is not mine own.

As soon as Paris has left, her speeches acquire a desperate urgency that makes Shakespeare, unusually in this play, run on over lines, and compress images in a way that he was not to do consistently until some time later in his career. After the macabre recital of the possible threats of the tomb, most of the rest of the scene is occupied by the Friar's melodramatic plan which emphasizes the pathos of Juliet's predicament most effectively.

I am nothing slow ... haste I am not anxious to appear cautious as it might make him diminish his haste.

Venus ... tears Love does not flourish where there is sorrow. There is also a quibble on astrology.

why it should be slow'd i.e. the fact that Juliet was already married.

to my face (1) openly (2) about my face.

it is not mine own She means that it belongs to Romeo.

Are you ... mass? A polite hint that she wishes to be alone with the Friar.

shield Forbid.

resolution i.e. that she will commit suicide.

presently Immediately.

Shall be ... deed Before my hand shall ratify another marriage ceremony (like a legal document).

both i.e. hand and heart.

long-experienc'd time Long lifetime of experience.

extremes Extremities of suffering.

play the umpire i.e. decide between them. There is a succession of legal images here – 'umpire'; 'arbitrating'; 'commission'; 'issue of true honour'.

arbitrating ... bring Deciding that which the authority of your years and knowledge could not arbitrarily settle.

craves as desperate an execution Needs action as desperate in carrying it out.

chide Drive.

cop'st Meetest.

thievish i.e. where thieves abound.

charnel-house At the side of every churchyard was a small building into which were placed bones that were found while digging the ground for further burials. They were stored in the charnel-house and periodically burned.

reeky shanks Leg-bones with an offensive smell.

chapless Lacking the lower jawbone.

distilling One that affects the whole body.

humour Fluid.

his native progress, but surcease Its natural progress shall all but cease.

wanny Pale and grey.

thy eyes' windows Your eyelids.

supple government The control which makes it supple.

stark Rigid.

against thou shalt awake In readiness for your awakening.

drift Purpose, plan.

inconstant toy Unsettling trifle.

prosperous Fortunate.

Act IV Scene 2

Preparations for the wedding indicate that the celebrations are not going to be limited to the few friends Capulet has mentioned in Act III, Scene 4, but that mourning for Tybalt has been forgotten. In the middle of this Juliet returns from Friar Laurence's cell and begs forgiveness of her father for her earlier opposition to him; his delight is such that he brings the wedding forward to Wednesday despite his wife's fears that there will be insufficient food. His generous, impulsive but tyrannical nature is once more emphasized.

Commentary

The start of this scene gives the action a stir by including the busy preparations for the wedding feast, and showing us Capulet still resolute in pursuit of his plans. Juliet's entry and request for forgiveness are clearly a surprise to him and further indicate his impetuous nature – his reaction is immediately to bring forward the date of the wedding. This tightens the action and means that Juliet has less time to brood over the possible effects of the potion. The dramatic irony of the scene is also increased, as the audience knows very well that Juliet's obedience is a pretence. We may note in Capulet's speeches how well Shakespeare is adapting his blank verse to the demands of colloquial orders given in a domestic situation.

cunning Skilful.
none ill No incompetent ones
'tis . . . fingers If he does not taste his own dishes he is not likely to be a good cook.
unfurnish'd Unprepared.
harlotry Minx.
How now, my headstrong! This does not seem to be the greeting of an enraged father; Capulet has regained his good humour.
becomed love Appropriate.
bound Indebted.
closet Room.
'Tis now near night The pace of the day has greatly accelerated, to tighten up the action and make the wedding more imminent.
They are all forth i.e. The servants are all out of the house.
reclaim'd Another metaphor from falconry; to reclaim a hawk was to recall it, or entice it back to the owner.

Act IV Scene 3

Juliet is preparing for bed and dismisses first the Nurse and then her mother, saying that she wishes to be alone. She prepares to drink the Friar's potion, but wonders first if the Friar has given her poison; next what will happen if she awakes in the tomb before Romeo arrives; and if the macabre surroundings of the tomb may move her to commit suicide. However, she resolutely drinks the liquid and falls senseless on her bed.

Commentary

The mood of this soliloquy is distinctly gothic in that it attempts to convey the chill of horror with all the apparatus of death and to show Juliet as, in her isolation, coming close to hysteria.

gentle Nurse When we remember that at their last meeting Juliet called the Nurse 'ancient damnation', it is clear that even to call her this, as she has always done, involves her in pretence.

orisons Prayers.

state i.e. of heart and mind as is evident from the next line.

cross Wayward.

behoveful for our state Necessary for our appearance at a public ceremony.

faint cold fear A fear that makes me feel faint and cold.

What should she do here i.e. What good should she be?

minister'd Prepared.

still been tried Always has been found to be.

healthsome Wholesome.

like Likely.

conceit Idea, fancy.

green in earth Newly buried.

like Likely.

mandrakes The mandrake is a plant with a forked root, and resembled the lower parts of a man. It was reputed to shriek if it was pulled up. This shriek supposedly had a fatal effect on the person who pulled it, or else caused him to go mad.

distraught Distracted, driven mad.

Environed Surrounded by.

joints Limbs.

spit i.e. transfix, as meat for roasting was impaled on a spit.

stay Stop.

I drink to thee She takes the Friar's potion as if drinking Romeo's health.

Act IV Scene 4

A short scene showing the preparations for the wedding.

Commentary

This scene echoes the start of Act I, and is well calculated dramatically to give the action a stir between scenes that both involve long speeches; the one before is concerned with fear, the one after with lamentation. The preparations go on all night, and the scene also covers the passing of night between Juliet's going to bed at the end of Scene 3 and the time for her awakening in Scene 5.

pastry The room where the pastry is made.
curfew bell The same bell that rings the curfew in the evening announces that it is first light.
cot-quean A man who interferes in matters that are normally a woman's concern. Some critics think that this speech should be assigned to Lady Capulet, as it is by no means certain whom he means when he says 'Angelica'. It is however to be expected that an old and trusted retainer would at the right time be on terms of familiarity with her master, and the Nurse earlier has been distinctly assertive.
watching Staying awake.
mouse-hunt (1) One who stays up at night (2) a womanizer.
I will watch you ... now I'll see that you don't do that now!
a jealous-hood A jealous woman.
I have a head ... logs (1) I am intelligent enough to find logs (2) I have a wooden head that will soon find logs.
loggerhead Blockhead (with pun from 'logs').
straight Almost immediately. In Shakespeare's time bride and bridgroom did not meet at the church but at the house of the bride so that he could take her to church.

Act IV Scene 5

At daybreak the Nurse goes to wake Juliet and finds her apparently dead. The preparations for rejoicing are quickly abandoned and lamentation becomes the order of the day; the entry of the Friar brings with it advice to all concerned to accept the death in Christian resignation. The scene ends with the Capulet domestics and hired musicians reflecting the general despondency.

Commentary

Much of the lamentation is distinctly mechanical, particularly that of the Nurse and Lady Capulet. Capulet himself speaks with rather more personality; the Friar in the usual terms of the formal tribute with encouragement to look forward to a better world. Many critics have commented on the badness of the last forty lines; they are scarcely appropriate at such a time and their wordplay is tired. Some have suggested that Shakespeare did not write the lines, but as an emerging writer for his Company of actors he was a victim of the convention whereby the Company clown would come onto the stage and deliver impromptu jests, sometimes not in the best taste.

Fast i.e. fast asleep.

your pennyworths Every minute, portion (of sleep) which you can.

set up his rest Determined, resolved; with a bawdy quibble. The Nurse reacts to the coming marriage in just the same way as she reacted when Juliet was preparing for her first meeting with Romeo.

'take you in your bed' and **'fright you up'** have similar bawdy meanings and the Nurse apologizes after having said the first of them.

Will it not be? i.e. Will you not wake up?

down again Lying on your bed again.

weraday Alas!

Accurs'd, unhappy . . . to my sight There is a purpose in the flat repetitive lamentation in that Shakespeare does not want the audience for a moment to think that the death is genuine; he is reserving his ability to move them until Act V.

In lasting labour In the never-ending struggle.

Beguil'd Cheated. Paris is thinking of himself, as does Capulet immediately afterwards.

Confusion's Destruction's, catastrophe's. In the next line the word has more its modern sense.

Your part i.e. Her body.

his part i.e. her soul.

her promotion (1) her happiness (2) marriage into the Prince's family.

'twas your heaven Your dearest wish (that she should gain higher rank).

rosemary see note p.40.

reason's merriment Our reason prompts us to rejoice (as she is now in heaven).

festival Festive.

office The reason they were ordered.

lour upon you for some ill Threaten you for some sin.

Move them i.e. anger them.

the case may be amended (1) the situation (2) the case for his instrument, evidently in bad repair.

'Heart's ease' ... 'My heart is full' These were both popular songs of the time.

merry dump A contradiction in terms as a dump was a sad song – perhaps indicating a certain lack of sensitivity in Peter.

soundly (1) thoroughly (2) in a way appropriate to musicians.

the gleek Jeer.

give you the minstrel A term of contempt as to call anyone a minstrel was to call him a good-for-nothing. See Mercutio's speech, Act III, Scene 1.

give you the serving-creature Call you a servant; 'creature' adds a note of contempt.

carry no crotchets Bear no insults, with a quibble on the musical crotchet.

re ... fa Notes on the scale, with implied insult.

note me (1) know what I mean (2) set it to music.

put out (1) extinguish (2) display.

dry-beat Beat you thoroughly without drawing blood.

When griping griefs ... silver sound Peter is quoting another popular song of the time.

Simon Catling ... Hugh Rebeck ... James Soundpost Presumably these are made-up names for the musicians, as they all pun on various parts of stringed instruments. Catling – a lute-string; Rebeck – a three-stringed fiddle; Soundpost – the peg inside the body of a stringed instrument.

sound for silver Play for money.

I cry you mercy I beg your pardon.

You are the singer i.e. and therefore cannot say anything.

have no gold Are not highly paid. He then completes the stanza he had started above.

Jack Contemptible rascal.

Revision questions on Act IV

1 Describe the meeting of Juliet and Paris at Friar Laurence's cell.

2 'I have a faint cold fear thrills through my veins'. Describe the fears of Juliet just before she brings herself to swallow the potion.

3 In what frame of mind does Capulet prepare for the wedding-feast?

4 Compare the reactions of the various characters who hear about the 'death' of Juliet in Scene 5.

5 What is the attitude of the various members of the Capulet

family to Friar Laurence in the course of this Act?
6 What is the *dramatic* reason for the foolery of the musicians?

Act V Scene 1

Romeo is in Mantua; his servant Balthasar arrives bringing news of Juliet's death and burial, but no letters from the Friar. Romeo then obtains some poison from a poor apothecary, intending to seek out Juliet in her tomb and to die with her there.

Commentary

This is Romeo's first appearance on stage since he left Juliet after their wedding night, and we find him in an optimistic frame of mind. In an ironic reversal of what has actually happened, Romeo has dreamt that he was dead and that Juliet came to revive him. The arrival of Balthasar reminds him that the stars are implacably against him, and his resolution immediately to seek out the dead Juliet to join her in death is a logical continuation of the love that fate has prevented from developing. The vivid description of the apothecary's shop is both atmospheric, melodramatic and closely observed.

flattering truth of sleep i.e. dreams that flatter us that they are true.
pressage Give promise of.
My bosom's lord i.e. love.
love itself possessed Love when one enjoys the real thing.
love's shadows Dreams of love.
Dost thou not bring me ... Juliet Romeo fires questions at Balthasar, who in the stage direction has come on 'booted' to indicate that he has just alighted from his horse. Romeo's questions indicate excitement and that some time has passed since he left Verona.
well i.e. at peace.
Capel's In Brooke's poem Capulet and Capel are used interchangeably.
presently took post Immediately rode by fast horse.
for my office As my responsibility.
Is it e'en so Romeo's desire to defy his fate gives a reminder of his slightly frenzied behaviour in the fight with Tybalt (III,1).
Hast thou no letters ... Friar A reminder of the earlier question, which indicates to the audience that the Friar's letters have gone astray.
means i.e. means by which I may lie with you.
tatter'd weeds Ragged clothes.

overwhelming brows Overhanging eyebrows i.e. with sunken eyes.
Culling of simples Picking medicinal herbs.
Meagre Pinched.
beggarly account Miserably small collection.
bladders i.e. to hold liquids.
packthread Stout thread.
cakes of roses Dried rose petals crushed together and used as a
 perfume.
Whose sale is present death The sale of which is punishable by
 immediate death.
caitiff Miserable.
forerun my need Anticipate my need.
forty ducats A large sum of money; a ducat was a gold coin.
soon-speeding gear Quickly-working substance.
utters Sells.
Need . . . eyes It can be seen from your eyes that want and oppression
 are killing you.
affords Provides.
break it and take this Break the law and take this money.
Put this in any liquid thing Romeo does not do so but drinks it as it
 is.
in flesh Better covered, i.e. grow fat.

Act V Scene 2

The bad luck that prevented Romeo from receiving the letter
from Friar Laurence is explained in this scene. His messenger,
Friar John, while looking for a brother who would accompany
him on his errand finds himself confined to a house where the
plague is suspected, and is unable to deliver the letter. Friar
Laurence is deeply disturbed and asks Friar John to obtain a
crowbar for him so that he may be in the Capulet tomb when the
time comes for Juliet to awake.

Commentary

The shortness of the scene means that it is almost entirely
functional in carrying the plot forward.

if his mind be writ If he has sent me a message in writing.
bare foot i.e. Franciscan. The Franciscans were enjoined to walk
 barefoot and friars usually travelled in pairs.
associate Accompany.
searchers People who in time of plague were appointed to view any
 dead body to find out the cause of death.

Seal'd up the doors The usual method of attempting to stop the plague from spreading involved locking the door and preventing entry or exit.

stay'd Stopped.

nice Trivial.

full of charge . . . import Full of news that was vitally important.

iron crow An iron crowbar.

beshrew me much Rebuke me.

accidents Events.

Act V Scene 3

Paris has come with his servant to strew flowers on Juliet's tomb, when they hear someone coming. It is Romeo, accompanied by Balthasar who is now sent off on an errand in order that Romeo be free to take his own life. However, as he opens the tomb, Paris steps forward and attempts to arrest him for having returned from banishment without permission. A fight develops and Paris is killed; only then does Romeo see who he is. Romeo enters the tomb, finds Juliet, takes the poison and dies. Just as the Friar arrives, Juliet awakes; he sees however that he has come too late and announces his intention of lodging her in a nunnery. Once she realizes that Romeo is dead, Juliet stabs herself with his dagger.

At this point the Watch arrives, summoned by Paris' page. They arrest the Friar and Balthasar and hold them until the Prince, the Capulets and the Montagues arrive in their turn. The Friar tells them what has happened and the Prince points out that the hatred of the two families has brought its own punishment in the deaths of their dearest children. A gloomy morning sees the two ancient enemies reconcile their differences and promise to set up the statues of the two lovers in pure gold.

Commentary

The earlier part of the scene is notable for the gothic horrors of the tomb, horrors that had been foreshadowed in Juliet's speech just before she takes the potion. A good deal of emphasis goes into reminding the audience that it is dark – Romeo does not notice who Paris is, for example.

The focus of the scene however is Romeo's last speech. This starts with his recognition of Paris as the man whom he has just killed but proceeds straightaway into a celebration of Juliet into which are combined many of the trains of images that have been so notable in other parts of the play. Here again is the light imagery which turns the tomb into a lantern, and talks of a lightning before death; the idea of Death keeping Juliet as his mistress; and that which compares Romeo's story to a sea voyage. After this, the remaining motions which finish off the play seem unremarkable.

stand aloof Stand a short distance away.
Under yond yew trees ... digging up of graves The details here set the scene and convey an atmosphere which one can only call gothic (yew trees, hollow ground, churchyard, graves).
lay thee all along Lie flat on the ground.
adventure Risk it.
sweet water Perfumed water.
wanting that If I lack that.
obsequies Rites performed for the dead.
keep Observe.
mattock A tool like a pickaxe, but with a narrow blade instead of a spike.
chiefly ... employment This is of course a ruse to remove Balthasar from the scene so that Romeo can commit suicide.
jealous Suspicious.
hungry churchyard i.e. because it had consumed so many bodies.
empty tigers Hungry and, therefore, savage tigers.
Take thou that i.e. a present of money.
despite Defiance.
Good gentle youth It is plain that though Paris recognizes Romeo, Romeo does not recognize him.
these gone The bodies resting in the tomb.
For I come hither ... myself i.e. because I've come here with poison to kill myself.
defy thy conjuration Reject your solemn appeal.
the Watch The town police force.
Did not attend him Was not paying attention to him.
triumphant Splendid.
lantern An architectural term meaning a turret with glass all round – like a lighthouse.
Death i.e. Paris.
a dead man Romeo is referring to himself.
keepers Jailers.
sheet Winding-sheet.
I still will stay I will always stay.
Will I set up ... rest I will remain here for ever.

shake the yoke The metaphor is that of a beast of burden coming home at the end of a day and shaking off his yoke.

A dateless bargain ... Death An agreement that will last for ever; a legal metaphor.

Come, bitter conduct ... guide Romeo is addressing the poison.

be my speed My guide and helper.

stumbled at graves It was thought that to stumble when taking a decisive step was a sign of ill omen.

unthrifty Unlucky.

I dreamt ... Balthasar does not want openly to admit that he had disobeyed his master's orders.

unkind Not of human kind; unnatural.

comfortable Bringing strength and comfort.

timeless Untimely.

O churl This is addressed to Romeo.

a restorative A medicine – which will cure her in that it enables her to join Romeo.

attach Arrest.

ground (1) earth (2) reasons.

circumstance Details of what has happened.

Stay detain.

mista'en i.e. mistaken its proper house.

his house His sheath.

Montague i.e. Romeo.

warns Summons.

down Dead on the ground between the tombs.

O thou untaught What bad manners!

To press ... grave A conceit which imagines Romeo pushing through a door before his father.

the mouth of outrage These bursts of passionate feeling.

ambiguities Events which are not clear.

spring ... head ... true descent Image of a river in the investigation of the events that have happened.

I be general of your woes ... death I will lead you in mourning and pursue those responsible, to death if necessary.

let mischance ... patience Submit to disaster with patience.

parties of suspicion Those people who are suspected.

Doth make against me Implicate me in.

both ... excus'd To accuse and to exonerate myself. Friar Laurence acknowledges that he can be accused of being the cause of the deaths, but he had no intention of so being.

in About.

date of breath Time I have to live.

their stol'n marriage-day The day of their secret marriage.

siege of grief The metaphor suggests that she was surrounded by grief (like a city) and could not escape from it.

borrow'd Temporary.

prefixed Planned, arranged.

closely Secretly.

Her Nurse is privy Her Nurse knows all about it.

some hour before his time Some time before my life would normally end.

still Always.

in post In great haste.

going As he went.

made your master Was your master doing.

make good Confirm.

therewithal Bringing the poison with him.

your joys Your children (followed by another example of antithesis).

winking at your discords Closing my eyes to your disagreements.

a brace of kinsmen i.e. Mercutio and Paris.

jointure A wife's marriage-settlement from her husband (or his Family): the opposite of a dowry which was the portion given by her *own* family. Capulet says that Montague's handshake – the ending of their strife – is all that he can ask from him for his daughter's jointure.

no figure at such rate No person will be so highly thought of.

sacrifices of our enmity Victims of our hatred.

glooming Gloomy. The final six lines are the last part of a sonnet.

Revision questions on Act V

1 What coincidences can you find during the course of this Act?

2 Describe the meeting of Romeo and Paris. Does Shakespeare make us feel any sympathy for Paris?

3 Compare the Friar's account to the Prince of what the audience knows already with that given by Benvolio in Act III Scene 1. Are both completely correct?

4 Give a close account of Romeo's last speech.

Shakespeare's art in *Romeo and Juliet*
Setting and themes

Setting

Romeo and Juliet is set in Verona, a city which, to the play's original audience, was remote and distinctly exotic. The Italy of the play in fact never becomes positively realistic for this reason; we hear that the 'day is hot' that the 'mad blood' is stirring; that the currency is ducats and that a pomegranate tree grows close to Juliet's window. The remoteness of Italy to the average Elizabethan meant that the country and its people appear in most Elizabethan plays in a distinctly stylized form, and the reputation of Italians was that they were small, dark and treacherous. This does not fit the romantic atmosphere that Shakespeare wanted to convey, and it is notable that even Tybalt does not in any way reflect the stereotype.

The setting is therefore in the main English rather than Italian; the puns of the language reflect a fashion that was very much an English one, and the young men who make them are what the Elizabethans would have called 'gallants'. The domestic scenes are taken straight from those that might be found in the household of a wealthy Englishman. Fires are lit and the Lord sees that there are enough dry logs. The kitchen staff are thrown into a frenzy by the demands made upon them to cater for a great occasion; servants are unable to read. The Nurse helps in the pantry, and the Lady has in her own keeping the key to the cupboard where expensive things like spices were kept. The entertainment is a masked dance (again very popular at the end of the sixteenth century), and the dance is held in the same room as that in which the feast takes place. After 'trenchers' 'joint-stools' and 'plate' have been cleared away, the tables are turned up, more torches are called for, and the fire is quenched as 'the room is grown too hot'. The dancers then begin to 'tickle the senseless rushes with their heels' – something they would be unlikely to do in Italy.

The two brawls are taken directly from the many similar fights that took place between bands of rival apprentices: 'Clubs' was their normal cry. On the wedding morning the bridegroom goes early to awake the bride in readiness for the ceremony and to serenade her before taking her to church. Wandering minstrels (as distinct from musicians) were of low repute in the England of the time, as since the advent of printing their services were of little account; Mercutio makes it plain that to imply that a man is a minstrel is to insult him. When he travels to Mantua Balthasar takes the quickest means of getting there, which is by post-horse. Friar John is prevented from giving Romeo Friar Laurence's message because he has lodged in a house that is affected by the 'infectious pestilence' and the doors have been 'seal'd up' – the duty of the constable in Shakespeare's time. The forces of law and order appear as the 'Watch' who arrive at the Capulet tomb by no means clear as to what is happening, but ready to arrest anyone there on suspicion. They are consistently satirized in Shakespeare's plays and in *Romeo and Juliet* they are portrayed even quite affectionately. The Apothecary's shop too is very English.

Themes

As we have seen, the story of *Romeo and Juliet* was old before Shakespeare was born, and its continuing popularity is the result of a theme that has appeal in all ages – that of young love. The youth and inexperience of the two lovers is constantly emphasized: Juliet is 'not fourteen' and Romeo is 'a virtuous and well-governed youth', and their mutual infatuation is such that each cannot stop thinking about the other. The freshness of this love is conveyed by original images taken from flowers, from light, and from religion. At the same time one is never allowed to forget that the love is threatened. Even when things are going well there is a sense of impending tragedy, a sense that such true and perfect happiness cannot last. The Prologue to Act I speaks of 'a pair of star-cross'd lovers' before the action of the play begins; Romeo has a deep fear of 'Some consequence yet hanging in the stars' that will bring 'some vile forfeit of untimely death' even before he has set eyes on Juliet. They have a deep feeling that their love will end in disaster, and Romeo comes to marry Juliet with a challenge to fate on his lips – 'Then love-devouring death do what he dare'. Juliet imagines Romeo descending into a tomb as he lowers himself from her window for the last time.

The love, then, is a consuming love, and in shortening the original time-scheme Shakespeare greatly increases the intensity. The atmosphere becomes one of passion and swiftness. Consuming love calls for *haste* (the other important theme). As soon as Romeo and Juliet have met, they want to get married, and the marriage is arranged for the next day. As the Nurse goes to tell Romeo of the arrangements Juliet is desperate in her anxiety that she is not returning as quickly as she might: 'From nine to twelve is three long hours', and when later she is waiting for night and Romeo, haste is all-important: 'gallop apace, you fiery-footed steeds'.

The Friar knows only too well the penalties of excessive haste; he says that 'these violent delights have violent ends' and urges Romeo to 'love moderately' – but the whole tenor of the play seems to be against him. It appears at the start that Verona is a powder-keg, ready to burst into explosive violence at the slightest confrontation of the two families, and it does so on two occasions; when it does, banishment immediately follows for Romeo, but he is equally hasty in his return to Verona, in the abruptness of his challenge to an interloper, and in committing suicide when his life suddenly seems not worth living. Similarly, Capulet is desperate that the match with Paris be finalized as quickly as possible, and Paris is scarcely less anxious for the same thing.

It is therefore all the more noticeable that when the frantic haste slows for a little, the calm interludes gain a great deal from the contrast; and that when the tragedy is complete the atmosphere is not particularly pessimistic, for the two families are reconciled by the lovers' deaths.

The characters

Romeo

But he that hath the steerage of my course
Direct my suit.

Italians have generally enjoyed a legendary reputation as lovers
and it would therefore be reasonable to expect Romeo to con-
form to this ideal. In fact Shakespeare's Romeo appears much
more English than Italian: fresh, inexperienced, and distinctly
maudlin at first, then full of the enthusiasm of one who has
made a new discovery. The soul of moderation in the face of
Tybalt's insults gives way to the rash but expert swordsman who
is plunged into the pit of despair on the news of his banishment.
Both in Mantua and on his return to lie with Juliet, he appears
impulsive yet with an air of innocence that keeps him attractive
as a person.

At the start of the play Romeo is absent from the brawl that
begins the action, but he is introduced soon afterwards in conversation with Benvolio. He is totally uninterested in recent
events as he has lost his heart to one of the beauties of Verona,
Rosaline, who remains as no more than an idealized love-object.
We never see her, and she is spoken of only in terms familiar to
anyone who has read other literature of the time, as the mistress
in the Petrarchan sonnet. This means that she is unapproa-
chable, is placed on a pedestal, and her admirer can only
worship her from a distance. It would interfere with the dramatic design were she to be brought on to the stage, as Juliet would
then have a competitor. Romeo's early speeches about Rosaline
show a love that is unformed and undirected; they are full of
clever antitheses:

Here's much to do with hate, but more with love.
Why then, O brawling love, O loving hate,
O anything of nothing first create!

These turn into the stronger contradictions of oxymoron:

O heavy lightness, serious vanity,
Misshapen chaos of well-seeming forms!
Feather of lead, bright smoke, cold fire, sick health . . . ! (I, 1, 173–8)

It is clear that Benvolio regards the Romeo who can talk like this with a measure of despair. After he has heard the conventional summary of Rosaline's obdurate chastity he decides to do something about it in persuading Romeo to attend the Capulets' feast in order to examine rival attractions.

When he next appears on stage it is en route for the feast and he is in company with Mercutio as well as Benvolio. This begins to show us another side of Romeo – what the Elizabethans would have called the 'gallant'. And though his self-pitying melancholy persists there are signs of the constant word-play that is so much a feature of Mercutio's speeches, except that where Mercutio is constantly bawdy, Romeo never is. We are clearly intended to think of him as more refined, and Capulet himself talks of him as

> a portly gentleman;
> And, to say truth, Verona brags of him
> To be a virtuous and well-govern'd youth. (I, 5, 65–7)

His behaviour at the feast suddenly shows us a new Romeo, who speaks with an imagery now taken from religion; equally ready to quibble on words, but with a new sensitivity expressed in the love sonnet used to convey the quality of this new emotion.

His speech as he observes Juliet shows this new urgency. The vital imagery of light is combined with language that for a formal situation is distinctly colloquial:

> Cast it off.
> It is my lady, O it is my love!
> O that she knew she were! (II, 2, 8–11)

When he has revealed himself to Juliet, he answers her practical and sensible questions with responses that show a degree of the abandoned delirium that he is later to display in Friar Laurence's cell. It is she who interrupts his meditation:

> It is my soul that calls upon my name.
> How silver-sweet sound lovers' tongues by night,
> Like softest music to attending ears.

with a recall to present realities:

> *Juliet.*   What o'clock tomorrow
>   Shall I send to thee?
> *Romeo.*   By the hour of nine.
> *Juliet.*   I will not fail.   (II, 2, 167–8)

He visits the Friar in this new mood and is spoken to in a kindly but patronizing way that shows him to be still very much a youth. The following scene, where he is reunited with his friends, gives us the only glimpse in the play of the normal Romeo. His pursuit of verbal quibbles is as relentless as Mercutio's, but his greater kindness is emphasized by the way in which he smoothes the Nurse's ruffled feathers. The marriage of the lovers may seem hasty — indeed the Friar gently hints that it is: 'These violent delights have violent ends.' But there is no doubt that Romeo and Juliet have a depth of feeling for each other that transcends anything else in the play.

The fatal scene of the fight with Tybalt shows us yet another side of Romeo and further emphasizes the impulsiveness that is part of his nature. He appears initially as the peacemaker, as his new-found alliance with the Montagues' traditional rivals gives him every reason to sustain such a role. He refuses to draw his sword even when such a refusal looks like cowardice and he cares little for what his friend Mercutio may think. Mercutio's death changes all that; it reveals the expert swordsman that up to now we have seen nothing of, and firmly emphasizes that Romeo is by no means deficient in manly attributes. He blames his misfortune on luck. 'O I am fortune's fool' is an exclamation that conceals the fact that some of the fault is his own.

Banishment brings out the worst in Romeo. With Juliet he had spoken and acted like a man; with the Friar he behaves like a spoilt child, throwing himself on the ground and tearing his hair in a frenzy. The Friar speaks for all of us when he says, 'I thought thy disposition better tempered.' The ring sent by Juliet acts with the Friar's lecture to restore him to a state of reason.

The second scene with Juliet is a good deal shorter than the first and is overshadowed by the added threat of Romeo's being put to death if he is found inside the city walls by morning. There is also the certainty of death at the hand of enraged Capulets if one of the Montagues is found on their territory. Once again Romeo is ready to stay, and it is the ever-practical Juliet who urges him on his way to Mantua.

Still impetuous in banishment, he believes without question the first thing he hears. His act in buying poison is decisive if ill-advised, and his vivid description of the apothecary's shop serves a necessary dramatic function while reminding us of his imaginative gifts in a slightly new direction. It is rather a surprise to find later that he has had time to write a letter to his father.

It is a feature of Shakespeare's mature tragedies that the hero is to a greater or lesser extent responsible for his own downfall; *Romeo and Juliet* stands rather apart from the great tragedies because the events of Act V are largely a result of bad luck. We can see in the character of Romeo some signs of responsibility for the tragic outcome in that he is always in a hurry. Had he taken more time over his actions, the tragedy would certainly have been averted, as indeed it would have been if he and Juliet had agreed to elope and to return when the fuss had died down. But this is to ignore one of the main features of all Shakespeare's plays – that he used a story first written down by another hand, and did not alter the essential ingredients. The catastrophe is therefore laid at the hands of fate or the stars. After Romeo has recognized Paris as the man he has killed he calls him 'one writ with me in sour misfortune's book'. Paris is of course the second man he has killed, but the emphasis of the play is never to indicate that Romeo is guilty for having done so, as in each case his opposite number had rejected words of peace and forced the encounter towards violence.

In the tomb Romeo regains the serenity, the passion and the sincerity that we have not fully seen since Act II Scene 2. He uses again his earlier imagery (Act II Scene 2), and as he shakes 'the yoke of inauspicious stars from this world-wearied flesh' we are reminded of his statement when on the way to the masque:

> for my mind misgives
> Some consequence yet hanging in the stars
> Shall bitterly begin his fearful date
> With this night's revels, and expire the term
> Of a despised life clos'd in my breast
> By some vile forfeit of untimely death. (I, 5, 106–11)

and that even when being married he has said to the Friar, 'Do thou but close our hands with holy words,/Then love-devouring death do what he dare'.

Juliet

> O, she doth teach the torches to burn bright.
> It seems she hangs upon the cheek of night
> As a rich jewel in an Ethiop's ear—
> Beauty too rich for use, for earth too dear.

The eternal paradox of Juliet is that she is supposed to be barely fourteen years old. In Shakespeare's source story she was sixteen, and Shakespeare seems to have made her two years younger in order to emphasize her youth and freshness. If so, it makes for formidable difficulties for anyone wishing to play the part today; it is rare to find a girl of fourteen with the necessary range and experience of love, while a superannuated Juliet accords with nobody's conception of the character. When one remembers that the original Juliet was played by a boy one wonders how accomplished Elizabethan actors generally were.

In her first appearance Juliet is presented to us as very much a little girl; completely dutiful in obeying her mother, blissfully unaware of the implications of the Nurse's earthy comments, though obviously quite used to hearing the embarrassing recitation of events of early childhood from affectionate but somewhat patronizing adults. She clearly is used to the idea of an arranged marriage – 'I'll look to like if looking liking move' – and quite ready to defer to her parents' judgement in this as in everything else.

She is at once different when she meets Romeo. Her conversation with him shows her using language in a way that is by no means bashful and retiring; instead she is able to play a game of verbal tennis with him, answering his conceits with ones that show her in no way his inferior. If her two couplets, on learning Romeo's identity, seem a little mechanical and contrived, her next appearance in Act II Scene 2 shows a tremendous development of character.

Here Juliet seems suddenly to have grown up; she is willing to stand up against her mother, her father and anyone else and this is one of the factors that give *Romeo and Juliet* the appearance of taking longer than the five days nominally occupied by the action. Her meditation about Romeo, 'What's Montague? It is nor hand nor foot/Nor arm nor face nor any other part/Belonging to a man' has a practical tone quite different from Romeo's speeches about Rosaline, something that is amplified when she starts questioning him:

How cam'st thou hither, tell me, and wherefore?
The orchard walls are high and hard to climb,
And the place death, considering who thou art. (II, 2, 62–4)

While Romeo relapses into a haze of ecstatic abandonment: 'I am afeared/Being in night, all this is but a dream,/Too flattering sweet to be substantial', Juliet is making arrangements for the visit to be followed up by using the Nurse as a go-between. It is she who calls Romeo back, not particularly to pay him more compliments but to fix a time for her messenger to meet him. At the same time Juliet is still modest and self-effacing, anxious that she should not be thought in any way wanton in her whole-hearted confession:

I should have been more strange, I must confess,
But that thou overheard'st, ere I was ware,
My true-love passion ... (II, 2, 102–4)

Indeed, her admission of her tendency to blush easily is a truly endearing feature of her character.

When the Nurse returns from seeing Romeo, we are shown the two sides of Juliet very clearly. The child who is anxious to tease information from a guardian who is tantalizingly ready to withhold it is also a girl who is growing in assurance: 'Where is my mother? Why, she is within/Where should she be? How oddly thou repliest.' Her deep sincerity comes out nowhere better than in the short speech just before her wedding: 'But my true love is grown to such excess/I cannot sum up sum of half my wealth.'

Juliet next appears waiting anxiously for night and the arrival of Romeo, ignorant of the fact that he has just murdered her cousin. Her speech is full of a subtle eroticism that shows her longing for physical union with him, but this mood is abruptly broken by the Nurse's entry with news of Tybalt's death. Juliet's reaction is at first to turn against her husband in obedience to the dictates of family allegiance, but when the Nurse condemns him she leaps to his defence, though with a feeling of desperation, and immediately hits on the truth: 'That villain cousin would have kill'd my husband.' Her repetition of the word 'banished' has a sort of frenzy about it very similar to Romeo's in the next scene.

When Romeo visits her for their wedding night, it is against the audience's knowledge that plans are afoot for her marriage to Paris, and that at any minute a visit from Lady Capulet is probable. Juliet is shown in a turmoil of emotions, first wanting him to stay as long as possible, then urging him on his way to Mantua to escape death. Lady Capulet's arrival is followed by a section with a great deal of word-play where mother and daughter are talking at cross-purposes, but the audience is aware of the double meaning of Juliet's speeches. Capulet shows that he is quite unaware of the way in which his daughter has grown up because he talks to her in the same bantering and patronizing way that one might use to a little girl – until he realizes that perhaps for the first time she will not fall in with his wishes. He immediately turns into a blustering tyrant who fulminates against her for fifty lines. The Nurse, unable to see any solution to the dilemma, advises Juliet to marry Paris; and she is left totally alone, needing for the first time in her life to put on a false front – to everyone except the Friar.

It is particularly interesting to see Juliet's treatment of Paris when she sees him at the Friar's cell. She is formal, correct and polite; the word-play has distinct similarities to that she had used with Romeo at their first meeting, but the imagery is not nearly as fresh, and as a result the speeches are totally without passion. Her enthusiasm for the Friar's desperate remedy is absolute and immediate.

As she prepares for bed after her apparent repentance before her father, Juliet's speech, once she has sent away the Nurse, reveals another side of Shakespeare's imagination, that in which he recreates the tomb. We have already seen signs of this as Romeo descended from her balcony earlier:

Methinks I see thee, now thou art so low
As one dead in the bottom of a tomb.
Either my eyesight fails or thou look'st pale. (III, 5, 55–8)

And now we have a series of gothic horrors retailed, and her speech increases steadily in emotional pressure as it proceeds to the actual taking of the potion.

By an unlucky series of accidents Juliet awakes in the tomb to find her husband dead beside her, and though the Friar has fulfilled his promise in being there to greet her when she wakes, he has failed, in that his plan has not worked. Juliet greets his wish to send her to a nunnery with horror; to a union such as hers, death is no impediment. Life without Romeo is equally unthinkable, and if death is a convention for ending a play when the author has nothing further to say, her suicide is paradoxically a consummation: 'O happy dagger./This is thy sheath. There rust, and let me die.'

In her loneliness Juliet has made us feel that we are close to true tragedy, and even in such an early play as this, where for the most part Shakespeare is honing his dramatic talent, hardly any character moves us as much as does Juliet.

The Nurse

And I might live to see thee married once,
I have my wish.

The Nurse is one of the most interesting characters in the play. Dramatically she is important as a contrast to the character of Juliet; coarse and bawdy where Juliet is naive and innocent and shallow where she is deep, but always warm and full of feeling where her young mistress is concerned. She is incurably talkative, repeats herself constantly and is fond of reminiscing; there is mild satire shown in the way that she, a servant herself, treats her own manservant Peter. She responds enthusiastically to the delights awaiting Juliet at the hands of any attractive male but she is unable to understand the depth of Juliet's feeling for Romeo; her advice to her young mistress faced with the dilemma of what to do in response to Capulet's order that Juliet should marry Paris indicates that her moral sense is slight.

We are introduced to the Nurse as the trusted household retainer, calling Juliet to see her mother in I, 3 in a very similar way to that in which she summons her for her planned wedding in IV, 5. She talks with total lack of inhibition, mentioning aspects of her private life that most women would prefer to keep private; the coarse joke that she makes about Juliet falling on her back – not in itself particularly funny – tickles her sense of humour enough to make her want to repeat it. The sexual side of marriage is a constant theme, as she keeps returning to it no matter how many times Lady Capulet attempts to head her off.

The Nurse's devotion to her mistress is enough to make her quite willing to go against the Capulets' wishes in furthering the development of Juliet's relationship with Romeo, and she has the force of character to argue that Romeo should not take advantage of Juliet's innocence. Her return to the eager Juliet is written to develop all the scenes's comic potential, as the information she carries is wrung out of her with allusions to the difficulties the trip has given her aching bones. Her reaction to the death of Tybalt is an emotional one and any member of the audience finds some difficulty in believing that Tybalt is the 'best friend I had'. Her use here is of course to act as one of the chorus that condemns Romeo and to prompt Juliet to a spirited and moving defence of her husband.

In her last two appearances she fills the audience with contradictory emotions. First she is ready to risk Capulet's wrath by standing up for Juliet against her father's command that she should marry Paris; later in the same scene her advice to Juliet to marry two men provides a most interesting comment on her own limited sense of morality and makes Juliet's role the more effective in leaving her quite alone. The Nurse's last appearance, discovering the 'dead' Juliet and then lamenting over her body, helps to provide the contrasting mood between the beginning of the scene and its end. The language she uses is stiff and unconvincing, compares badly with Capulet's 'death lies on her like an untimely frost' and is an entirely consistent indication of her limitations as a person.

Mercutio

A gentleman, Nurse, that loves to hear himself talk, and will speak more in a minute than he will stand to in a month.

In Arthur Brooke's poem, Mercutio is a courtier, mentioned several times by name but having no direct part in the action. The development given by Shakespeare to this sketchy character is most notable; he becomes Romeo's friend and a man so remarkably similar to him in some ways that it is clear that he is used as a dramatic sounding-board – for Mercutio stays the same throughout the play whereas Romeo develops a great deal. It has often been remarked that Shakespeare had to kill him off in the middle of Act III because, with his liveliness and vivacity, he is already much more interesting than Romeo and threatens totally to eclipse the hero. This is however to ignore the fact that Romeo has depths that Mercutio is incapable of understanding or rivalling.

We are introduced to Mercutio when Romeo and Benvolio are on the way to the Capulets' feast. He is shown as being scornful of the legendary ability of lovers to escape from earthbound things; indeed he soon introduces what is to be his constant theme, that of the bawdy side of sex. His speeches are amongst the bawdiest in all Shakespeare's plays, and a close examination of many of them would even now shock those whose belief is that the story of *Romeo and Juliet* is an example of perfect romantic love. There is of course a purpose in all this, for if Romeo has to listen to extremely personal remarks as he does in Act II, Scene 1 he never responds in kind; in that sense the immature Romeo has already grown beyond the range of a Mercutio.

To understand Mercutio fully we have to be as agile verbally as he is, because more than anyone else in the play he uses puns. To an Elizabethan it was the sign of a quick wit to be able to see different meanings in the same word – 'a wit of cheveril, that stretches from an inch narrow to an ell broad', and it is so characteristic of him that he puns compulsively, even after he has received his death-wound; 'Ask for me tomorrow and you shall find me a grave man' perhaps indicates that he is faced with something serious for the first time in the play. True, he ruefully acknowledges Tybalt's ability as a swordsman in calling him 'more than Prince of Cats', but at the same time there is a good deal of the compulsive jester about the manner of his challenge to Tybalt, mixed with conventional ideas of honourable behaviour that for Romeo are irrelevant.

For most of the time Mercutio speaks in prose that is vigorous and characteristic. It enables Shakespeare to use a constant stream of colloquialisms: 'Without his roe, like a dried herring' . . . 'Good Peter, to hide her face, for her fan's the fairer face' . . . ''tis not so deep as a well, nor so wide as a church door, but 'tis enough'. But in the scene in which Mercutio is first introduced he speaks in verse that is only marginally less energetic. The situation is used to give the character an emphasis that it does not have elsewhere, for the speeches here have an imaginative quality particularly notable in the famous 'Queen Mab' speech. Though this is ultimately based on the techniques of rhetoric taught in Elizabethan schools – it takes a single idea, that of a dream being a chariot driven through the mind of a sleeping man, and elaborates it systematically – it does so with great originality. As a commentary on events of the time it is mildly satirical, when Mercutio remarks on the ladies' breaths that are tainted with sweetmeats, it returns to mild bawdry before Romeo silences him. Only the Prince has a speech of comparable length outside Romeo and Juliet themselves, and there is no doubt that anyone who has seen the play will remember Mercutio for this if for nothing else.

One of the most interesting scenes in which he appears is his encounter with the Nurse in Act II Scene 4. She is of course his counterpart in the scenes which involve Juliet, in that she too has a comparatively shallow nature and her idea of love is as limited as his. To bring them together is therefore instructive; he has the advantage of her in that he is in company with his friends while she has only Peter in attendance on her, but he still shows up rather better than she does. Mercutio's humour is at first apparently irrelevant – 'A sail! A sail!' – then hints at the Nurse's appearance. He goes on to make suggestive remarks about her relationship to Romeo and her morals generally, and her indignation is such that we notice her venting her ill-humour on Peter.

In his development of Mercutio, therefore, we can see Shakespeare's ability to create memorable characters who are more than mere devices to show up others in the play.

Capulet

God's bread, it makes me mad!

Capulet and Mercutio are the two most interesting minor characters in the play. In Capulet we are shown an authoritarian Elizabethan father, a wealthy head of a household whose word is law in his own house and who shows a testy hot temper if any should be presumptuous enough to question it.

We see him first as the reasonable man and father who, after calling for his sword to join in the fight with the Montagues with no less enthusiasm than he had done many times before, answers Paris's request to be allowed to woo Juliet with a kindly, paternalistic attitude that tells Paris not unkindly that she is as yet too young, and that he should wait for two years more before she is old enough to marry. One of his virtues is not that of consistency, because he forgets this readily when it suits him to do so; and though this is partly in the interest of dramatic tightness, there is evidence elsewhere that he is impulsive.

At the feast he is the perfect host, talking nostalgically with his old cousin about their long-past dancing days. He is tolerant, prepared to ignore the entry of one of the Montagues to the festivities, and even ready to call him a 'virtuous and well-govern'd youth'; only after Tybalt's insistence that the intruder be exposed do we first see the other side of Capulet that becomes more prominent as the play progresses – indeed there is some irony in the fact that he rebukes Tybalt for wanting his own way, something he himself wants when we see him confronted with Juliet's refusal to marry. When the time comes for departure, he emphasizes the further attractions that are available in order to detain his guests as long as possible: 'Nay, gentlemen, prepare not to be gone,/We have a trifling foolish banquet towards.' By this stage, then, the audience thinks very highly of Capulet: he has been sensible enough not to want his daughter to marry too early; firm enough to impose his will uncompromisingly on the ridiculous Tybalt; tactful enough to turn a blind eye to Romeo's uninvited entry to the feast; and he has been a warm-hearted host.

Capulet is then off stage for nearly two whole acts and when he reappears his dramatic function has significantly changed. In planning the marriage of Juliet and Paris he has forgotten all the good reasons he put forward in Act I for delaying the match. There are enough hints in the earlier part of the play for audience and reader to realize that his nature can be peppery; now it becomes volatile, and he threatens to react violently at the slightest hint of disobedience from his daughter:

> Mistress minion you,
> Thank me no thankings nor proud me no prouds,
> But fettle your fine joints 'gainst Thursday next
> To go with Paris to Saint Peter's Church,
> Or I will drag thee on a hurdle thither. (III, 5, 151–5)

The way he turns upon the Nurse for coming to her Mistress's defence confirms him as a petty tyrant: 'Peace, you mumbling fool!'

This notion is further strengthened when the wedding feast is in preparation. Here Capulet is ready to consider no other point of view than his own, bringing the wedding forward by a day and thus clearly inconveniencing the arrangements of his own household. He is also forgetting the original plan in which the wedding was to have been a quiet one, with 'no great ado, a friend or two' because of the recent death of Tybalt. All this is now conveniently forgotten, and the scale of the celebrations calls for 'twenty cunning cooks'. The old Capulet of Act I reappears briefly during the preparations: 'Mass and well said! A merry whoreson, ha.'

When the 'dead' Juliet is discovered he is given the most

telling lines. In Act I he has talked of 'fresh female buds'; one of them is now covered with an 'untimely frost' and in continuation of the word-play: 'Flower as she was, deflowered by him.' His last speech in the scene is rhetorical and slightly mechanical in its effect:

All things that we ordained festival
Turn from their office to black funeral:
Our instruments to melancholy bells ... (IV, 5, 84–6)

In the final scene he says but little. He is the first to hold out his hand to Montague to end the quarrel that had cost both families so much. He is a memorable character but his role is always to give background atmosphere or to throw the story of Romeo and Juliet into sharper relief.

Friar Laurence

We still have known thee for a holy man.

Everyone in the play speaks well of the Friar; he is trusted by Montague and Capulet, by the Prince, and by Paris, no mean achievement in the Verona of the play. At the same time he is essential to the progress of the plot for he not only marries Romeo and Juliet, but his is the idea of using his knowledge of herbs to prepare the potion that will solve Juliet's problem for her; and it is only by a series of unlucky accidents that his plans are frustrated.

Friar Laurence is a Franciscan, as we hear several times in the course of the play. This means that he is not attached to a monastery but goes about preaching and living on charity. Shakespeare's conception of his position somewhat confuses it with that of the parish priest. We first find him picking the herbs which are the raw materials of that specialized knowledge so vital to the story, and moralizing rather obviously on their application to man:

Two such opposed kings encamp them still
In man as well as herbs: grace and rude will (II, 3, 23–4)

He treats Romeo somewhat patronizingly at first, supposing that his fire has melted the glacier of Rosaline's chastity, only to be told of the urgency of Romeo's new conquest. The fact that the whole scene is written in rather laboured couplets tends to deprive it of much urgency, but the audience can appreciate the truth behind his comment on Romeo's late and unlamented affair: 'For doting, not for loving, pupil mine.' His hope that in consenting to marry the two lovers he will heal the long-established rancour between the two families ultimately proves to be naive, at least in the short term; we feel that he is well-meaning but not very sensible. His age is emphasized in order to increase the impact of Romeo's youth, but he is well able to understand the power of the attraction that the lovers have for each other. His comment on their love: 'These violent delights have violent ends' is to prove only too true within two acts, but he is young enough to comment on Juliet's rushing to meet Romeo that:

A lover may bestride the gossamers
That idles in the wanton summer air
And yet not fail (II, 6, 18–20)

– an unusually poetic image for a Friar to use.

When the news of Romeo's banishment arrives, the Friar is able quickly to bring him to his senses and to change black despair into something like resolve. His decisive advice is quickly appreciated by the Nurse: 'O lord, I could have stay'd here all the night/To hear good counsel. O, what learning is'.

To deal with Juliet's desperation requires rather more ingenuity, and in this his knowledge of the properties of plants we have been told about earlier makes him propose the solution of a drug that will give the appearance of death for forty-two hours. His description of the ordeals that she is likely to face in the tomb has more than a touch of melodrama about it.

The catastrophe of the last act is, as we have seen, caused by bad luck; the failure of Friar John to deliver the letter to Romeo; Romeo's own early arrival at the tomb; and the speed with which he carries out his intention of suicide. In the face of this the Friar can only comment: 'A greater power than we can contradict/Hath thwarted our intents', and his final very long speech is to inform the other characters of the facts which the audience already knows.

The Friar is, in himself, not a very 'dramatic' person: he is constantly referred to as 'kindly', and such people are seldom exciting. But the part he plays in the plot *is* highly dramatic; he is thus one of the most important characters in the play.

Minor characters

Lady Capulet

> By my count
> I was your mother much upon these years
> That you are now a maid.

Lady Capulet is much more slightly drawn than her husband. This may be in part because she is so much younger than he, as we are able to calculate her age as being about twenty-eight. As all parts for women were played by boys it is clear that it would be much easier for a boy to act a woman of twenty-eight than it would be for him to act one much older. Her relationship to her daughter appears a formal one; Juliet answers a summons to see her mother with 'Madam, I am here', and throughout the scene she contrasts notably with the much more relaxed Nurse. It is she who presents her daughter with the idea of marriage in a style of studied formality: 'Verona's summer hath not such a flower', and her description of Paris continues in this vein, using the image of a book that is so elaborate that it threatens to collapse under the weight of its own ingenuity: 'This precious book of love, this unbound lover,/To beautify him only lacks a cover.'

When she appears next immediately after the death of Tybalt, it is to make an equally mechanical call for revenge on the Montagues: 'Prince, as thou art true/For blood of ours shed blood of Montague.' This stiffness continues in Act III Scene 5 when her desire for vengeance is further expressed in a plan to poison Romeo in Mantua. Here her dramatic purpose is to act as a foil to Juliet, who speaks in terms of ambiguity which the audience understand very well; her role at such a time cannot be sympathetic and the character develops hardly at all. She resolutely supports her husband in his plan to hasten the marriage with Paris: 'Talk not to me, for I'll not speak a word./Do as thou wilt, for I have done with thee.'

A slight degree of personality is given to her in her relationship with Capulet: 'Ay, you have been a mouse-hunt in your time', but when the 'dead' Juliet is discovered her words have no more individuality than those of the Nurse, and distinctly less than her husband's.

Finally we have her exclamation on finding Juliet bleeding in the family tomb: 'This sight of death is as a bell/That warns my old age to a sepulchre.' These words suggest a person who is rather older than twenty-eight, and are an indication that Shakespeare was not taking a great deal of interest in the character; they are plainly inconsistent with the Lady Capulet of Act I, and show that in a new situation Shakespeare is using what is effectively a different person. Few in the audience would be likely to remember, and no one could have imagined that the plays would be subject to minute scrutiny four hundred years later.

Benvolio

I do but keep the peace

We are told that Benvolio is Romeo's cousin; in Elizabethan terms this means merely that they are related. He is clearly one of the Montagues, in that Tybalt is more than ready to pick a fight with him in the first scene of the play, but if Tybalt is constantly associated with violence Benvolio is the exact opposite – a peacemaker: 'Put up your swords, you know not what you do.' He is the nephew trusted by Montague to give an unbiased account of the brawl in the first scene, and the youth later trusted by the Prince to give an unbiased account of the second brawl, in which both Mercutio and Tybalt are killed. Yet it is made plain that at no time is Benvolio cowardly, for on each occasion he draws his own sword in an attempt to prevent the quarrels from becoming dangerous.

While we never see Tybalt in anything other than a rage, Benvolio is developed rather more because he is Romeo's friend as well as his cousin and, together with Mercutio, is used to draw out the various features of Romeo's character. After his vivid description of the fight he introduces a new element to the play – the element that is to become its main characteristic – poetic quality:

Madam, an hour before the worshipp'd sun
Peer'd forth the golden window of the east . . . (I, 1, 116–17)

This may be a conventional way of describing daybreak, and expressed in a way that is rather flat, but it prepares us for, and contrasts with, Romeo's much more original use of the same light imagery an Act later. On Romeo's entry Benvolio is seen as the yardstick of what is sensible – if a little earthbound – and he makes Romeo's modish melancholy seem as forced and artificial as it undoubtedly is. His conversation with Romeo is briefly interrupted by the short scene between Capulet and Paris, but when the conversation is resumed his comment is accurate and prophetic: 'Compare her face with some that I shall show/And I will make thee think thy swan a crow.'

In the scene on the way to the feast Benvolio says but little, as the greater impact comes from Mercutio; whenever the two of them are together, which happens regularly, his retiring nature is eclipsed by Mercutio's outrageous and very bawdy punning. But he shows himself more than ready to join in the game of words with an intentional malapropism: 'She will endite him to some supper.' After implicitly criticizing Mercutio for his extrovert and slightly aggressive attitude, he suddenly finds himself in yet another threatened brawl – one which, despite his efforts, becomes only too real. The last we see of him is when he gives only a slightly biased account of the fight between Mercutio, Tybalt and Romeo – biased because he omits the part played by Mercutio in provoking Tybalt. Perhaps the account is as complete as might reasonably be expected in the circumstances, but once his dramatic function is complete Benvolio is immediately dropped from the play.

Tybalt

What, drawn and talk of peace! I hate the word.

Mercutio has a good deal to say about Tybalt, and all of what he says is amply reflected in what we see of him. 'A duellist, a gentleman of the very first house' is here a character who never appears in the play except in a context of violence. He is ready to lead an active pursuit of the family feud in the first scene; to expose Romeo as an intruder in the gathering at Capulet's house; to fight anyone who gives him the slightest occasion; and in particular to challenge Romeo to the fight that results in Mercutio's and his own death. Because each of his appearances is brief, the character never becomes anything more than a sketch, and a crude one at that.

There may be an element of satire in the portrait, as Mercutio and Benvolio have little time for the affectations of men obsessed by the latest fashions in speaking and in fighting: 'Why, is not this a lamentable thing, grandsire, that we should/be thus afflicted with these strange flies, these fashion-mongers . . .?'

The pun they make on his name, connecting him with Tybert the King of Cats, fully expresses their contempt, and it is significant that even after he is dead he is never mentioned except in the context of the violence by which he has lived: 'That villain cousin would have kill'd my husband' and 'Tybalt, liest thou there in thy bloody sheet?'

Paris

Verona's summer hath not such a flower

Lady Capulet's comment on Paris tells us a good deal about him. There is no doubt that he is an approved suitor; the way the Nurse echoes her comment indicates that he is physically attractive, and there is equally no doubt that he is a little conventional.

We are introduced to him as one of the earliest characters in the play as he asks Capulet for his daughter's hand, clearly considering that fourteen is by no means too young to be married. Capulet's request that he wait for two years seems to us reasonable, but one scene later we find Lady Capulet mentioning the proposed match to Juliet with no hint that it will be as long as two years before the marriage takes place. He is asked to woo her, but we are never shown him doing so, perhaps because for all his vital importance to the plot, Paris never becomes more than a background character.

At his next appearance in Act III Capulet informs Paris that there has been no time to persuade his daughter to be married. In view of the haste with which the action is pressing forward it is not difficult to believe this, but it conceals the fact that Shakespeare is clearly thinking that more time has elapsed since the last scene; he is already operating a double time scale, something he was to do more extensively ten years later in *Othello*. Paris's role in this scene is very small; he simply reacts to what Capulet says, and shows understandable enthusiasm that the wedding is to be brought forward: 'My lord, I would that Thursday were tomorrow.'

Dramatically, this puts much more pressure on Juliet, and it might have been tempting here to make Paris into something of a villain. Shakespeare however does not do so; we find Paris talking to Friar Laurence at the start of Act IV absolutely correctly – tactfully withdrawing when he feels that his presence is not appropriate. But as the victim of ironic answers from Juliet (like those given to Lady Capulet in the scene before), we see that he is the only person in the theatre who does not understand the double meanings.

At the report of Juliet's death he does no more than to echo the general rhetorical woe; his lengthiest part is reserved for that in front of the Capulet tomb, where his sincere lament for Juliet cannot be allowed to compete with Romeo's, (which appears fifty lines later), and therefore seems flat.

It is clear that his position in the play is such that Paris cannot be made too attractive, except in places where it does not matter. Within these limitations he is made to appear likeable and courageous.

The Prince

The Prince is a figurehead rather than a character. He makes three appearances, each one following on some disturbance which he has to stop and on which he has to deliver summary judgement. We gather in his first speech that there have been three riots before the play opens, which would suggest that his commands have little effect. This, however, is not the impression we gain from the play; all characters treat the Prince with deference and indeed apprehension.

His lament at the end: 'See what a scourge is laid upon your hate' seems spoken more in sorrow than in anger, and to have implications that his role is closer to a divine than an earthly ruler. He certainly does not appear in any way inadequate, and his power is suggested by commanding and rhetorical language.

Style

Sonnets

Romeo and Juliet is one of Shakespeare's earlier plays. This means that its memorable features are most frequently those we would associate with the works of his apprenticeship – and Shakespeare was famous as a poet before he achieved fame as a playwright. Before he had written *Romeo and Juliet* he had written numerous sonnets and two long poems which achieved great success, *Venus and Adonis* and *The Rape of Lucrece*. Many of the features of these works reappear in the play. Sonnets in themselves are seldom really dramatic, and it is therefore a little surprising that at their first meeting Romeo and Juliet fall naturally into a sonnet: 'If I profane with my unworthiest hand/This holy shrine, the gentle sin is this.' The sonnet continues as far as, 'Then move not, while my prayer's effect I take,' and Juliet immediately starts another, which is interrupted by the Nurse.

There are several other sonnets: or, rather, part-sonnets. Benvolio talking about love (I, 2, 45–50); Romeo talking about Rosaline (I, 2, 90–95), Paris speaking at the Capulet tomb (V, 3, 12–17) and the last speech of the Prince (V, 3, 304–9) are examples of part-sonnets, while the Prologues to Acts I and II are complete ones. Formality of language, then, is one of the constant feature of the play, but it is one of Shakespeare's characteristics that he neatly sidesteps excessive formality and suddenly becomes vitally original. So the stale language of the Petrarchan sonnet used to describe Rosaline suddenly becomes the reinvigorated language used for Juliet.

Language

The normal language of the play is the *iambic pentameter* – the decasyllabic line of blank verse. Though it had only been invented thirty years before *Romeo and Juliet* was written, and was then an attempt to imitate Latin hexameters in English, by 1590 it had become the accepted form. Shakespeare manages to use this form with remarkable variety. The language of the Prince is rhetorical and similar to that used by many contemporary playwrights:

Rebellious subjects, enemies to peace,
Profaners of this neighbour-stained steel– (I, 1, 79–80)

These two lines say the same thing three times, and as all Elizabethan schoolboys had lessons in rhetoric, it is interesting to see various examples of different rhetorical techniques appearing; one of these is *antithesis*, where one idea is balanced against another: 'She is too fair, too wise, wisely too fair' or 'Here's much to do with hate but more with love/Why then, O brawling love, O loving hate.' Another technique is the use of *oxymoron*: 'Feather of lead, bright smoke, cold fire, sick health', or 'Dove-feathered raven, wolvish-ravening lamb!'

Imagery

One of the vehicles for conveying the originality of the play is the quality of its imagery, and the dominating image is light. It appears in many ways: the sun, the moon, stars, lightning, fire, exploding gunpowder, lanterns; and then to contrast, the opposite, night, dark, rain and clouds. Juliet speaks of Romeo as 'thou day in night'; he speaks of her as the sun rising in the east. They make the stars seem insignificant, and taking the old cliché that Juliet's eyes are like stars, Romeo gives it new life by letting his imagination exaggerate the idea:

Two of the fairest stars in all the heaven,
Having some business, do entreat her eyes
To twinkle in their spheres till they return. (II, 2, 15–17)

This is just the start of a flight of fancy that continues for another five lines. As Romeo prepares to depart for Mantua he speaks of the 'envious streaks' which 'lace the severing clouds in yonder east'. He comes to Juliet in the tomb, which he calls 'a lantern' – which makes 'this vault a feasting presence, full of light'. There are many more examples of imagery in the play which are similarly developed such as the idea of life being a voyage, and Death being a lover.

Word-play

A feature which it is difficult to overlook is the amount of *word-play*. To us, the *pun* is perhaps a somewhat juvenile means of conveying humour but in the sixteenth century it was a great deal more than that. It was the means by which any speaker could convey the quickness of his wit, and if the person to whom he was speaking was unable to follow the train of thought, it reflected badly on him. 'Can you not conceive?' says Mercutio to Romeo when he is a little slow in seeing a double meaning. This is why nearly every character in the play puns constantly, sometimes at moments we would consider scarcely appropriate. If we allow the fact that Mercutio is so devoted to word-play that he puns as he is dying – 'Ask for me tomorrow and you shall find me a grave man' it is rather harder to accept that Romeo in a moment of deep emotion should say 'Flies may do this, but I from this must fly' or that Juliet should say:

> that bare vowel 'I' shall poison more
> Than the death-darting eye of cockatrice. (III, 2, 46–7)

To examine the different levels of meaning in the play's various puns brings the reader surprisingly close to the mind of the time – and some of these puns he might find mildly shocking.

Couplets

There are undoubtedly features of the play that are difficult for a 20th-century playgoer to accept. One of these is the considerable part played by scenes written in couplets. There is some evidence that Shakespeare came to realize this himself, as in his later plays he uses them much less and even in those written two or three years later couplets are used only to end scenes or movements. Indeed in *Hamlet*, written perhaps five years after *Romeo and Juliet*, we find a scene written in couplets used to make fun of that outmoded way of writing. Another tedious feature is perhaps the rhetorical lamentation given to the Nurse and the Capulet family on the discovery of the 'dead' Juliet; here the characters' speech is a reflection on the type of person who is speaking.

Dramatic irony

Shakespeare seems to have had a particular feeling for dramatic irony, of which there is a good deal in the play. This is when the audience knows what the true situation is or is likely to be, and the character who speaks the words does not. Thus Juliet is apparently agreeing with her mother that vengeance must be taken for Tybalt's death, but the audience knows that her real meaning is different. As Romeo leaves Juliet to go into exile, she says:

Methinks I see thee, now thou art so low,
As one dead in the bottom of a tomb (III, 5, 55–6)

little realizing that the next time she sees him he will really be dead in a tomb.

Prose

Shakespeare makes extensive use of *prose* in the play. His usual custom was to use prose for lower-class characters, but he does not always do so in *Romeo and Juliet*. After his whimsical and extravagant 'Queen Mab' speech, Mercutio speaks mostly in prose, and as his speeches are composed largely of quibbles this is not surprising. One cannot but notice the difference between his language and that of the Nurse; Mercutio is constantly giving us evidence of extreme mental agility, while the Nurse's is repetitive, colloquial and frequently goes off at a tangent. The serving-men of Act I and the musicians of Act IV (both categories no doubt played by the same actors) are different again.

Experimentation

Above all, in *Romeo and Juliet* one is aware that Shakespeare was experimenting. Some of the things he does in this play he was soon to abandon or alter; his lines were gradually to run on more and to have fewer punctuation marks at the end; and his imagery was to become much more dense. But for all the stylistic faults of the play and its excessive reliance on coincidence, it was immediately, and has remained, a great poetic success.

General questions plus questions on related topics for coursework/examinations on other books you may be studying

1 What developments do you notice in the characters of Romeo and Juliet between Act I and Act V?

Suggested notes for essay answer:

1 *Introduction*
(a) Idea of play is to show development of a love affair and its final development into catastrophe (i) once love has matured, threat is from external sources (ii) greatest development must therefore be in first half of play.

2 *Romeo*
(a) At start his love unfocused (i) means by which this is conveyed – Petrarchan attitudes (ii) means by which this is expressed – mainly linguistic (antithesis, oxymoron etc).
(b) Tremendous change on meeting Juliet – note use of imagery.
(c) He is still basically impetuous and adolescent (i) e.g. reaction when he hears of banishment (ii) decision to go to the tomb and his behaviour there.

3 *Juliet*
(a) At start a little girl (i) way Nurse speaks of her (ii) way she reacts to suggestion of marriage.
(b) Change that occurs in her at feast (i) her practical reaction even in balcony scene (ii) nervous excitement at return of Nurse from seeing Romeo.
(c) How she surmounts difficulties posed by Tybalt's death (i) her resolution when faced with marriage to Paris (ii) deepening of her love which continues into tomb.

4 *Conclusion*
Both characters develop though Juliet more so than Romeo (i) her development continues until end of play (ii) Romeo of Act V has much in common with Romeo of Act III.

2 Describe the chapter of accidents which led to the deaths of Romeo and Juliet.
3 Where did Shakespeare draw the material for *Romeo and*

Juliet? Point out and comment on any additions or alterations made by him.

4 Write an essay on the structure of *Romeo and Juliet*.

5 What is the importance of the family feud in the play?

6 'O! I am Fortune's fool.' Do you consider this to be a fair assessment of Romeo?

7 In the Prologue Romeo and Juliet are described as 'star-cross'd lovers' and reference is also made to their 'death-mark'd love'. Does Shakespeare create the impression that their death is brought about by a cruel overwhelming Fate, by sheer accident or by their own wilfulness?

8 'My dismal scene I needs must act alone.' What is the dramatic value of the lack of sympathy between Juliet and the other people of the Capulet household?

9 Write a character sketch of Mercutio, noting carefully what he says about himself and what others say of him.

10 Write a character sketch of the Nurse, showing in what ways she provides comedy and relief.

11 Can the character of Capulet in Act III be reconciled with his character in Act I?

12 Do you consider the Friar to be wise, honest, foolish or an underhand schemer? Refer closely to the text in your answer.

13 Compare and contrast the characters of Benvolio and Tybalt.

14 Write a detailed analysis of any two soliloquies in the play.

15 How far does the reconciliation at the end of the play make a good ending?

16 Show from *Romeo and Juliet* how Shakespeare varies his poetic effects to suit different dramatic situations.

17 Write an essay on Shakespeare's use of metaphor and simile in *Romeo and Juliet*.

18 Write an essay on the use of dramatic irony in this play.

19 Does the continual punning increase your enjoyment of the play or do you consider it overdone? You should quote from the text in support of your views.

20 Why do you think *Romeo and Juliet* has remained a popular play on the English stage?

21 'These violent delights have violent ends.' Show how the suddenness and violence of the love of Romeo and Juliet are brought out in the play.

22 Describe a love affair in any book you are studying which ends sadly.

23 Write about a novel you have read in which fate or coincidence plays an important part.

24 Sometimes the minor characters in a book influence events. Examine any two minor characters in your chosen book and show what part they play in its action.

25 Describe an incident in which unnecessary violence is used in a book you know well.

26 Give an account of the effects of conflict in a play or a story.

27 Compare any two lovers in a novel you have read with Romeo and Juliet.

28 Write about a character whose humour contributes to your appreciation of a book you have read.

29 Describe the relationship between parents and children in a particular book.

30 Show how atmosphere is created through the use of images in a book you have read.

31 Take a setting that is outside Britain in a book you are familiar with, and write a letter to a friend describing it in detail.

Further reading

The Arden Shakespeare: Romeo and Juliet, ed. Brian Gibbons (Methuen 1980)

Romeo and Juliet, ed. T. J. B. Spencer (Penguin, 1967)

The Sources of Shakespeare's Plays, K. Muir (Methuen 1977)

Shakespeare's Tragedies: An Anthology of Modern Criticism (Penguin 1963)

Shakespeare's Wordplay, M. M. Mahood (Methuen 1957)

Shakespeare's Imagery, Caroline Spurgeon (CUP 1965)